SoberPowers

How to enjoy sobriety,
live your best life, and not
be weird about it

Drew Millar

"I now have freedom. I am back in control and have regained my self-respect. I am not locked in a battle for sobriety. I drink as much as I want, whenever I want. The truth is I no longer want to drink. I see now that alcohol is addictive, and I had become addicted . . . I've never been happier. I am having more fun than ever. It's as if I have woken up from the Matrix and realized that alcohol was only dulling my senses and keeping me trapped rather than adding to my life."

(Annie Grace, This Naked Mind)

CONTENTS

INTRODUCTION

BREAKTHROUGH

"I can't believe my drinking has come to this," I thought, reaching for my phone. It was time to confess. I hadn't been showing up to work, and my boss knew something was wrong. I was in full blown survival mode. It was time to set things straight.

That day, I was reeling. My nerves were racked from constant anxiety. My head was spinning. The buzzing in my ears made it feel like I was being electrocuted. In short, I felt like absolute shit. I was on the tail end of another week-long bender, and I had to minimize the damage. "I had done this before though, right?" Not exactly. At this point, everything had caught up to me. And people had caught on to me.

The excuses wouldn't work anymore. This way of life wouldn't work anymore. People were fed up, and so was I. Reaching for that phone in utter desperation was my rock bottom.

That was three years ago.

It's All Fun and Games, Until It's Not

Looking back, I didn't have much reason to become addicted to alcohol. As far as I know, it doesn't run in my family. I didn't even start drinking until college. But a decade of serious boozing and living amidst a heavy drinking culture left me vulnerable. It also gave me social anxiety and a habitual method for dealing with it. And that habit got out of control. By the time I was 30, I needed booze for almost every occasion. Good or bad, a drink (or 20) made life go down more smoothly. Until it didn't.

I'm not gonna lie—drinking was fun for a very long time. I owe the early parts of my career to being able to hang out and connect with my more established colleagues. I had countless adventures while under the influence, none of which would have happened if I had been sober. I was good at drinking. I enjoyed drinking. And I was in control of it. Until the day came that I wasn't. But I didn't see it that way at the time. Alcohol played such a seemingly positive role in my life, it was hard to admit when it started to drag me down.

Like any bad habit, my drinking progressed. What started as "just a bad hangover now that I'm getting older," mutated into something sinister. There came a point when I could no longer control my drinking. I would frequently black out. The next day, my anxiety and stomach ache would be so bad that only another drink would get me out of bed. Sound familiar? I still remember those terrible mornings, lying in bed, ready for the day to be over. Promising myself that "this would be the last time." As the day began, I'd reach for some booze to calm my nerves. Other times, I'd count literal minutes until my anxiety would hopefully subside. It never really did. I was trapped in the world of active addiction, and it wasn't a fun place to be. I'm guessing you can relate.

Pretty soon, my life was like being on a never-ending roller coaster. I was either drunk or hungover. But none of it was really all that fun. The more regular my withdrawals became, the more my life suffered, and the more my problems accumulated. My girlfriend of three years broke up with me because she was tired of me being overly emotional and hungover all the time. Can you blame her?

Next, my health started to decline. Only a couple years prior I was the best CrossFit athlete at my gym. Now I could barely get out of bed. I had aches and pains all over my body, and I was tired all the time. And don't forget about my failing career. Like I said, I could barely make it to work on time, and my boss was at his wit's end with my behavior.

"Holy shit, what had happened to me?" I tried to answer this as I lay awake in bed, staring at the dizzying whirl of my ceiling fan, anxiety shooting through my body, dehydrated from another day spent consuming poison. The trajectory of my life, which once looked so purposeful and bright, was no longer clear to me. I couldn't envision any real future for myself. I was stuck in a dangerous place, and it felt like I was barely hanging on.

On the Wagon, SoberPowers Included

Well, that painful phone call was my first step out of rock bottom. I finally admitted to another person what for years I hadn't been able to admit to myself: That I was drinking way too much and that I couldn't stop. That I couldn't take it anymore. And that this way of life would no longer work for me. Sure, I was still hounded by social anxiety and shame. And yes, I physically felt like crap if I went a few days without booze. And no, I couldn't imagine a social life without drinking. My life was undoubtedly in shambles, but I had to make a change.

And so, I quit drinking. As I write the words on this page, it's been over two years since I made that decision. Trust me, that seems about as crazy to me as it probably does to you. Two years ago, alcohol played a major role in almost every aspect of my life. I couldn't socialize without it. I couldn't manage stress without it. I couldn't fall asleep or wake up without it. I couldn't have gone two days without it, let alone two years. Today, my life is totally different. I am on a new trajectory and alcohol plays absolutely zero role. Truly, after a decade of "normal drinking" followed by a few more years of destructive self-sabotage, I hit the cold, rough, and slimy slab of rock bottom. It wasn't a fun place to be, and I still cringe when I think about it. But I returned to the surface alive and sober. But that's not all…

Along the way, something else happened. Something even better. You might even say something miraculous. *I found a new path to sobriety. A path that has improved every aspect of my life.* An approach that has filled me with a renewed sense of gratitude and purpose. I found an enjoyable and meaningful way to move forward. I didn't just get sober. I also *gained my SoberPowers*, improving both my mindset and lifestyle in ways I could have never previously imagined.

So what are SoberPowers? And what does it mean to have them? And how the hell did I get sober? Well, you'll have to read on because that's the purpose of this book. To give you an idea of what it's like to have SoberPowers, I am now mentally and physically healthier than at any other time in my life. The anxiety that used to haunt me is gone, and I look better than ever before. I wake up every day energized to pursue my deepest passions and ultimate purpose. And I have the focus to move my life forward in any way that I choose. None of this was possible when I was a drinker. To top it off, I rarely think about alcohol anymore. I don't miss my drinking days one bit. I truly love being sober and the positive lifestyle that comes with it. At the end of the day, there are hundreds of possible ways to "achieve sobriety." But to truly love the decision and thrive as a sober person, you need to have SoberPowers.

Equipped with SoberPowers, you are not merely sober. You are living your best life. And it works in both directions. Gaining SoberPowers will undoubtedly help you achieve sobriety in the short term, but it will also make your sober lifestyle worth it in the long run. So that you never have any doubts. My SoberPowers have given me a renewed sense of purpose in life. And if you read on, I'm convinced *the same will happen for you*. If you doubt this, I understand. Two years ago, I would have doubted me too. In fact, you and I probably have more in common than you think.

"WINNING"

When I first started on this path of sobriety, I felt the same as you are probably feeling right now. Scared. While sitting at rock bottom, I remember watching a TV show that dealt with the subject of alcoholism. I was almost embarrassed to hear the "A word," and I was filled with shame. "I wasn't one of those guys, was I? I wasn't an alcoholic, right?" I was ashamed to find myself addicted, and I couldn't imagine a life without drinking. It felt like a lose-lose situation: either keep drinking and dig to an even deeper rock bottom, or get sober and lose everything I *thought* I knew about life. I mean really, how do you go on a date without drinking? Forget dating, how do you even have friends if you can't go out for drinks? How do you go from being the life of the party to being that *creepy sober guy*? To be honest, I didn't know how to move forward. I didn't see any worthwhile paths to sobriety. So I didn't know if I'd make it. But then, something crazy happened.

I found out that I wasn't in a lose-lose situation at all. I quit drinking, but I didn't lose my life in the process. I found out that most of what I thought I knew about alcohol and sobriety was brainwashing and lies. Now that I know the truth, I don't miss drinking at all, and I don't consider myself an alcoholic. I've moved on, and I'm free. Sure, things look a bit different now, but the changes are all positive. The truth is that I've gained so much more than I ever had in the first place. I gained my SoberPowers, improving my life in just about every possible way. Physically and mentally, I'm on top of my game. I'm living according to my own values and following my deepest passions. Every day, I'm moving forward, and I'm truly thankful for that fateful moment when I had to admit my drinking problem to my boss. *What seemed like rock bottom was actually an opportunity to grow and change.*

And that's what this book is all about. Maybe you feel like I did two years ago—desperate, looking for a way out. Or maybe you just want to reevaluate your relationship with alcohol. Maybe you just want an improved and more meaningful lifestyle. Either way, I want you to know that your current situation is anything but a losing one.

Waking up the first morning after truly committing to sobriety was one of the best moments of my life. I had committed, and I knew the alcohol-induced sickness and anxiety were gone for good. As I lay there in bed, I felt gratitude for the first time in years. I felt motivated. And I've felt the same way every morning since. On top of that, I see past the brainwashing. I see both addiction and sobriety for what they really are. And here's the thing.

Achieving sobriety is not easy...but it can be much easier than you think. And despite the rough patches you will inevitably encounter, it can be altogether enjoyable. You'll see as you keep reading. You'll also see that I didn't go from Drunk AF to a full blown SoberHero overnight. My path is strewn with bumps, mistakes, and unexpected obstacles, but I'm truly thankful for every one of them. Even today, with all the progress I've made, I still get questions from people. They ask me if I'm doing okay. In truth, the past two years have been the best of my adult life. They've been more formative than any time I can remember. They've also been the most productive and fun. The same could soon be true for you.

Most importantly, I don't think of myself as an alcoholic. No doubt, I used to be a hardcore alcoholic, but those days are long gone. *I'm not addicted anymore. With my SoberPowers, I moved on and rarely think about drinking.* Alcohol has absolutely zero power over me. So how could I possibly be an alcoholic? You wouldn't call someone who quit smoking two years ago a smoker, would you? Why is it so hard for ex-drinkers to move on? Even if it were true, a label like that wouldn't do much for us anyways. So no, you do not need to refer to yourself as an alcoholic once you have your SoberPowers. That part of your life will be over. And like me, you'll be free.

Your New Life: Happy, Healthy, Purposeful

So yeah, I'm two years into this new way of life. Two years living with SoberPowers. And to be honest, I don't miss anything about my old ways. Not even close. Not even the kinda fun days before my drinking took a dark turn. I really don't miss any of it, as my new life provides me with so much more. Here are just a few of the many positive benefits I've experienced:

- My physical and mental health have improved dramatically. As a drinker, I was fat. As a sober person, I've lost 30 pounds *and* added muscle to my frame. My performance as a CrossFit athlete, despite being 34 years old, is at an all-time high. I find it much easier to avoid junk food and have replaced those empty calories with nutritious meals. And I finally have a healthy and consistent sleep schedule. After getting my usual eight hours of sleep, I wake up early. And I wake up with gratitude and motivation to meditate and work on myself. Doesn't that sound better than waking up with a hangover? Or feeling a sense of dread first thing in the morning?

- My confidence and social life have leveled up. I used to think drinking alcohol created my social life. After all, what would you do with other people if you couldn't go to happy hour or grab drinks? In a surprising shift, I now see that it's the exact opposite. At the time, I was worried about being the *creepy sober guy*. Now, I realize my real problem was being the *creepy drunk guy* for all those years. People are hardly themselves when under the influence of alcohol, and I was no exception. Now, when I hang out with people, I'm really me. I remember and enjoy everything. I truly connect with others and on an even deeper level. I have gained an amazing sense of confidence because I no longer need a drink to enjoy a date or an evening out with friends. How terrible a feeling it was to be in my thirties and still needing to pregame with a bottle? My social life has improved dramatically during the past year. I'm closer to my family and friends than ever before. I have the courage and social skills to go out and meet new people. And I haven't been to a happy hour in over a year. With SoberPowers, you can do the same.

- I'm way more productive now, and I'm finally getting after the important things in my life. From a work perspective, my drinking days were rough. How many days I wasted just sitting at my desk hungover, unable to think critically or strategically. And I'm a project manager, so imagine how that went down. Now that I am mentally focused all of the time, my work life is better than ever. I'm truly productive every day, and my stress levels have dropped off as I now have the mental capacity to deal with issues as they arise. No more waiting until tomorrow, or next week, while my body detoxes. On top of just having my regular job in order, I now have the time to pursue my passions. For the first time in my life, and after years of procrastination, I'm finally working on the things that are most meaningful to me. And it fills me with energy every day. You'll see what I mean as you start on this path for yourself. Being sober saves you a lot of time. Think how much time you wasted drinking and being hungover. Replace that with healthy routines and fulfilling work, and your career will improve in leaps and bounds. You'll see.

These are just a few of the many benefits I've experienced since gaining my SoberPowers. And they are all game changers. But my favorite part of being sober is that *I'm no longer a slave to a drug*. I think you know what I mean, right? Thoughts of drinking used to dominate my mind.

Before a night of drinking, it was . . .

What type of alcohol will be served at the party?

How can I limit myself to one drink per hour?

If I overdo it, how will I get home?

The next morning, it was . . .

How much money did I spend last night?

When will this hangover go away?

What is that buzzing in my ear and pain on my side?

How much time and energy are wasted with this endless mental banter? It's impossible to know until you become sober for yourself. But believe me, a quiet and focused mind is one of the greatest SoberPowers of them all. You'll see. I don't have to manage my drinking intake because there is no intake. I don't have to worry about how to get home because I am always able to drive. I don't have to check my bank account in the morning because I stay hydrated with water for free. I don't worry about drinking anymore. And I don't think about alcohol. *I am free.* And that is by far the best thing that has ever happened to me. If you stay with me for the rest of this book, you'll get to experience this for yourself.

On top of this freedom, I no longer have hangovers. I repeat, I have not woken up dehydrated, anxious, or sick for the past two years. There hasn't been a single day that I had to slog through just to get to bed with the hope that I'd feel better the next day. My life used to feel like one giant hangover. During my darkest years, hangovers would sometimes last three days—*three days*. And that would happen every week. What a way to live your one precious life, huh? Well, those days are long gone. I make the most of my time now and feel great just about every day. There really are no off days (or weeks). To someone who has never struggled with drinking, that might not sound like a big deal. But for people like you and I, eliminating hangovers is a game changer, and another SoberPower to add to your repertoire.

Dazed and Confused

As you will learn in the coming chapters, getting sober is really not that complicated. Not when you go about it the right way. It can also be a fulfilling and enjoyable experience. And believe me, I know some of you are shaking your heads at me right now. But stick around and you'll see what I mean.

I will say that the most difficult part of this can be the social stigma. The stigma of being that *creepy sober guy*. In mainstream society, quitting drinking means that you have issues. It means that you did too much of something that is assumed to be okay as long as it's done in moderation. Not only is "social drinking" deemed acceptable, but it is praised and glorified (see half the commercials on TV). That's why some people assume that you have a drinking problem when you no longer drink. How messed up is that? People view the path of sobriety as difficult and the destination as unsatisfactory. But stop to think about it for a moment. Does this really make any sense? What's wrong with the decision to stop consuming poison and start improving your life? Since when is being healthy and in control a bad thing? Ah, but the stigma persists.

As crazy as all this sounds, it is nobody's fault in particular. People are just victims of the massive amounts of alcoholic brainwashing. And it's everywhere. Beer companies tell us that drinking is cool, and that if we show up to the party with a case of cold ones, we'll draw women like bees to honey. Wine connoisseurs tell us that drinking is sophisticated and that learning to identify 234,568,805 types of wine will turn us into intellectual icons. And then there are the recovery groups like Alcoholics Anonymous. Their brainwashing tells us that achieving sobriety is difficult, and that even if we succeed, we'll miss out on one of the true pleasures of life. That we are forever sick and forever alcoholics. This brainwashing is serious stuff. And like I was two years ago, you are most likely a victim right now. But don't worry, that's about to change. We'll take care of it in the coming chapters.

Why You Might Just Love This Book

The purpose of this book is to turn this brainwashing on its head, and then to turn sobriety into a positive experience for you. Best of all, this book will give you something no other sobriety method can: an awesome lifestyle totally removed from alcohol. And by totally removed, I mean you won't even think about sobriety all that much after a while. You will see that you give up nothing when you quit drinking. And that everything you think alcohol does for you is bullshit. And you won't have to call yourself an alcoholic. Your past life will have no control over you, and you'll be free. You will be mentally and physically stronger than ever before. And you'll be improving every day. This is living life with SoberPowers.

Of course, I can't guarantee that all of the above benefits will happen to you right away. But I can guarantee you will finally be on the path to better health, happiness, and success. I have no idea where my life is going to take me. But I know beyond a shadow of a doubt it's a better place than it would have been if I had kept on drinking. So, if you're thinking about what you have to *give up* to become sober, I want to challenge you to drop that, and think about all you have to *gain* from taking this path.

CHAPTER 1

BEER ME

"Medical researchers are correct that the brain changes with addiction. But the way it changes has to do with learning and development—not disease . . . The many addicts who end up quitting do so uniquely and inventively, through effort and insight. Thus quitting is best seen as further development, not 'recovery' from a disease." (Marc Lewis, The Biology of Desire[1])

Just two years ago, alcohol played a major role in my life. By age 32, I had a legit drinking problem, and you'd be right to guess that this didn't happen overnight. Like so many others, it all started in college. It was then that I found out that booze made me happy. Later on, I discovered that alcohol removed my social anxiety, stress, and feelings of not being good enough. Sounds like a recipe for disaster, right? I was done for. I was caught in the trap. And my drinking gradually got worse from there.

I'm a statistical outlier. If you're waiting for a childhood confession about sneaking bottles from my parents' bar, you'll

---

1 Lewis, Marc. *The Biology of Desire.* PublicAffairs, 2015.

be disappointed. Growing up, alcohol wasn't a big part of my parents' lives. It wasn't a factor in mine either. I had a healthy childhood. My parents did a good job raising me and my siblings. We grew up playing sports, had lots of friends, and went to great schools. I have no traumatic memories. Only positive ones that I still look back on with joy. At this point, you may be wondering, "Wow, Drew, congrats on the great childhood, but I had all kinds of drama and difficulties growing up. I barely made it out alive!" You're not alone. Like I said, I'm the outlier here. According to the "experts," this never should have happened to me.

But this just shows the sneakiness of alcoholism. To be honest, if your childhood was rough, I give you a lot more credit than I give myself. I was the worst kind of alcoholic because I had so many advantages in life. I had no reasons. No warning signs. So I couldn't blame anyone but myself. But honestly, that's not even the point.

The point is that we are all in this together. Alcohol is a physically addictive drug, and we all got hooked somehow. It doesn't really matter what happened in the past. What matters is whether we learn from our mistakes and move forward. My story proves that enough brainwashing and bad decisions can make anyone vulnerable. But it also proves that learning the truth and building good habits can lead anyone to freedom.

This is Normal, Right?

After my fun (and sober) childhood, I entered the world of adolescence. I drank every once in a while at parties in high school, but I don't remember ever being drunk. Once I got to college, things changed. It was there that I got my first real taste of heavy drinking, and that's how it went for the next four years. But that's "normal," right?

It sure seemed like it, so I joined a fraternity. In case you're not familiar with how college fraternities work, imagine being welcomed with open arms into a community of binge drinkers. I still remember our "open tap" initiation parties where all 25 of us pledges had to finish multiple kegs without ever closing the tap. Talk about chugging. Talk about blacking out. Needless to say, we all ended up puking and passing out on the snowy sidewalks of our campus. As perverse as it seems now, my fraternity made drinking seem cool. I fit right in.

Upon graduating from college, I started working for a company with a booze-oriented culture. Getting drunk at team parties was encouraged. Showing up to work hungover was permitted. And then there were the factory trips to Asia where heavy drinking was practically expected. The work days on those trips were fairly innocuous, but things took a wild turn at dinner. Think ten plus drinks every night of the week. Think company-expensed open bars. Imagine drunk karaoke. Imagine waking up barely remembering what country you were in. That was my working life. As crazy as it sounds, working in this culture made drinking seem like a good career move. I fit right in.

At age 26, just a year into my career, I moved to Amsterdam as an expat. Lucky me, right? If you don't know, Amsterdam is one of the major party cities on the planet. There, I met people from all over the world who drank and partied just like me. So I drank my way through 20 European countries, and at the time, it seemed like a blast. Drinking was an international pastime that had the power to connect people from all over the globe! Again, I fit right in.

Seems like a normal way to spend your twenties, right? Nobody ever told me to slow down or stop. I didn't think there was any problem with my lifestyle at all. I was living it up. But that's when some toxic undercurrents started to form.

A Storm is Brewing

Looking back, I absolutely couldn't imagine life without alcohol in those days. Everyone was drinking and partying like me. It all seemed completely normal. So by the time things started going downhill, I never thought to blame my drinking. Not at first anyway.

The first sign was when I began relying on alcohol to navigate me during social situations. But that's what alcohol is for, right? That's what I used to think. And this meant I was soon drinking at every social event. Call it mild social anxiety, or call it introversion, but it wasn't easy for me to enjoy the company of others. Being fun and social didn't come naturally to me back then. I often found myself second-guessing my actions or worrying about the "right" way to act in certain situations. If you can relate to this, you know how exhausting it can be—to have a constant diatribe of negative self-talk scrolling through your brain like the credits to a bad movie.

But I found comfort in a six pack, and I used alcohol as a replacement for natural confidence and social skills. Alcohol turned the volume down on my monkey chatter and self-judgement. And that's how drinking became a habit for me. Before long, going into social situations without a buzz felt like marching into battle without armor. And my "social drinking" worked. I was the life of the party, and I made a lot of friends in the process. But relying on alcohol as the only means to do this is like taking steroids to hit a home run. Sure, it feels good at the time, but it's not real. It doesn't make you more confident. It doesn't improve your social skills. And for me, that was just the start of the problem.

Breaking Every Rule

After a few years of living and boozing overseas, I was ready to come back home. I was also about to turn 30. If you're doing the math, that's nearly a decade of heavy drinking and partying. I remember thinking that this was the time to cut back on the booze. I wasn't exactly a kid anymore, and I was about to be out of my twenties! Not that alcohol was causing a lot of harm in my life back then, but it was definitely holding me back from realizing my true potential. I rarely felt my best. My hangovers were regular and only getting worse. But I still didn't think I had a "problem." I figured everyone felt this way and I could always just cut back, right?

So being the "highly functioning problem solver" that I was, I made plans to "manage" my drinking. To start with, I'd only drink on weekends! I'd only have two drinks an hour! I'd always make sure I was good to drive home. I bet you can guess a few more of my drinking management rules. I bet you can also guess how well I kept them. Maybe you can even relate with the shame I felt on Sunday nights: barely remembering the weekend I'd just stumbled through, regretting how much money I'd blown, kicking myself over how many of my "rules" I'd broken. The more I tried to manage my drinking, the more aware I became of how much trouble I was really in. Ring a bell?

As I said, I drank to excess and blacked out quite frequently during my twenties. I partied and made tons of bad decisions. I let alcohol get in the way of my own health and wellness. And trust me, I'm definitely not claiming any Man of the Year awards here. *But despite all the bullshit effects of my heavy drinking, I never really thought I had a drinking problem.* To be fair, I would put "drinking less" at the top of my list of goals for each year. But when I failed to achieve it, I didn't think much of it. I knew my life and health would improve dramatically if I slowed down my drinking. And I knew it would be better to feel comfortable in my own skin rather than use alcohol as a social medicine. But I didn't really examine myself until I started breaking all those damn drinking management rules. That's when I first started feeling like I was letting myself down. That's when I started to suspect that I was out of control.

Looking back, I now know that I had a drinking problem for many years. But I had always been able to "control" it. I could still show up to work on Monday morning. I could still do my part in maintaining personal relationships. And I even made it to the gym a few times per week. Plus, every drinker around me seemed to be balancing the same things. So drinking never seemed like a big deal. But I soon learned that people with drinking problems are just one setback away from driving their life off a cliff. I thought I was okay because I could keep up with the people around me. But my own drinking habit was like a pile of gasoline-soaked wood—one spark of drama or personal crisis could set off a five-alarm fire and burn everything down. And that's what happened. When my life went up in flames, it went up *fast*. It still shocks me to this day.

Hello Rock. Hello Bottom.

It was the summer of 2016 when my girlfriend (from my Amsterdam days) of three years joined me in the USA. I was 30.

We had just spent a year maintaining a long-distance relationship, so the stakes were high. We had a fun relationship in Amsterdam. We travelled together and were both very active. Needless to say, things had changed a bit during our year apart. I had changed. I was drinking more heavily than ever before.

Our date nights weren't fun anymore. I would frequently drink to excess and provoke fights. The next day wasn't any better as I'd wake up with yet another hangover. Then I started showing up tipsy to the activities we used to enjoy so much. Sounds like a fun guy, right? The worst part was I brushed it all under the rug. I acted like it was my little secret. But she knew. You can't really hide a heavy drinking habit. When you look like a zombie, smell like an outhouse, and slur like a sailor, people figure it out.

My girlfriend didn't put up with this for very long. It also didn't take long for me to realize that she was interested in other people. The circumstances of our breakup hit me like a kick to the stomach. It tore me up. For the first time that I could remember, I felt physically sick, even when I wasn't hungover. I remember sitting at my desk and trying to focus. Anxiety gnawed at my nerves. Negative emotions flooded my psyche. I couldn't think. I couldn't work. I didn't know what was wrong with me. But every day was filled with this terribly nervous feeling of dread and self-doubt. I wasn't myself anymore, and it scared the hell out of me. Up until then, I could blame most of my bad days on hangovers. But I couldn't kick this one. The anxiety was there day after day. Lucky, or so I thought, I had alcohol to make me feel better.

And of course, drinking really did make me feel better. It made me feel like myself again. I still remember sitting down at home after an unproductive, anxiety-racked day and taking my first sip of beer. It was like all my problems were washed away by that first drink. I could think again. I could breathe again. It was crazy. *I didn't know that alcohol had that kind of power until I started self-medicating with it.* I could be having the worst day ever, trapped in a vicious loop of bullshit monkey banter, and all it took was a few drinks to set my mind straight. At least for a couple hours. But since I was tired and desperate, drinking seemed better than wallowing in misery for the rest of the evening. I was no longer drinking for fun or to connect with others. I wasn't even drinking to manage my social anxiety or deal with everyday stress anymore. I was using alcohol to feel like myself again.

The more I drank, the worse my life got. Just as I had done for the past ten years, I was still going hard at nearly every social event. And I was still getting obliterated on weekends. But that was just the start. Now, I was also drinking in between social events. I was drinking after work. And I was drinking alone. Alcohol was almost always in my system. My energy level was declining. My career was suffering. Nothing was making me happy anymore. By 2017, things were really getting bad.

At that time, I was 31 and had been drinking heavily for well over a decade. I'd had countless hangovers over the years, but now, they were different. I started waking up to panic attacks. I'd head to work with my face so swollen I couldn't even look people in the eyes. I had pain in my sides, and my blood pressure shot up to dangerously high levels. And emotionally, I was destroyed. Both my anxiety and depression spiked to levels I'd never before seen. I was getting no enjoyment out of life. I was barely hanging on.

Any normal person would assume this was when I finally decided to quit drinking. But I was "ambitious." I started drinking in the morning. That made my hangovers go away. And it temporarily calmed down the worst parts of my anxiety. But it also meant I was drinking around the clock. That's when things finally spiraled out of control. I started to miss work, many times without even calling in. I passed out during Thanksgiving with my family. I fell off the grid with my friends. I was going down, and looking back, I don't think I realized it. I'd always thought I could cut back if I really needed to. But now, when I needed to quit more than ever, I couldn't.

The summer of 2017 was the worst ever. I was stuck in a dreadful cycle: drink to excess, have terrible withdrawals, and finally feel decent after a few days. Only to rebuild my confidence, go out with friends, and set the pendulum swinging back in the other direction. I couldn't stop. My entire life was now tuned to the rhythm of addiction. I kept missing work. I got fat. I started having severe kidney pain. A constant ringing in my ears followed me at every turn.

One day towards the end of the summer, I was in the midst of another bender and had missed yet another day of work. Things were already awkward between me and my boss, and I couldn't believe I'd put myself in this situation again. I'd repeatedly promised myself to stop. I remember thinking, "Can I really not control my drinking anymore? Has it finally come down to this?"

All the evidence was saying "no." I was scared to lose my job. I was terrified for my health. I couldn't live like this anymore. Something had to change.

A New Beginning

I made that change on a Tuesday morning. I woke up knowing I had to do something to save my job. So I did the unthinkable and called my boss. I told him that I was having issues with drinking, and that I was going to get help. Little did I know at the time that I was also saving my life. That was my first look upward from rock bottom. It was the worst I'd ever felt, and the most humiliated

I've ever been. Looking back, I still don't know how I mustered the courage to make that phone call and end my nightmare. But this nerve-racked, sweat-soaked alcoholic could still dig deep. And digging deep was what lifted me out of rock bottom. But it wasn't just the end of my nightmare. It was the beginning of something great.

CHAPTER 2

ALL THE BRAINWASHING

"Once we begin to realise that we are hooked on alcohol and that the physical addiction is easy to overcome, why do we find it so hard to quit? It's because we believe that we are making a genuine sacrifice and are actually 'giving up' something worth having. We feel mentally deprived when we stop. This feeling of deprivation is the real problem because even if you do not drink for years, but believe that you have 'given up' a genuine pleasure, then the feeling of deprivation and misery will last the rest of your life." (Jason Vale, Kick the Drink . . . Easily!²)

Alcohol kills. It may be easy to forget amidst the Bud Light King's antics and our country's opioid crisis. But more people are addicted to alcohol than all the other hard drugs combined. The goal of this book is not to go into all the details of the massive problem our country faces regarding alcohol. This book is about you, me, and our path forward together. But that said, it would

---

2 Vale, Jason. *Kick the Drink . . . Easily!* Crown House Publishing, 2011.

be irresponsible of me not to mention some of the data. A few hard facts:

- Every year, alcohol is the cause of 5.3% of deaths worldwide (or one in every twenty)[3].

- About 300 million people throughout the world have an alcohol use disorder (almost 4 percent).

- Approximately 88,000 people die as a result of alcohol every year in the United States[4].

Can you believe that we advertise this stuff to our children? Apparently, Americans are drinking more now than before Prohibition was enacted[5]—you know, the time when alcohol was made illegal owing to the horrible effects it was having on society. According to Dr. Tim Naimi, an alcohol researcher at Boston University, "Consumption has been going up. Harms (from alcohol) have been going up. And there's not been a policy response to match it."

So yeah, people are boozing more these days. It's a massive problem and our leaders aren't doing much about it. Just think about the role alcohol has played in your life. I showed you what it did to me. And as you can see from the numbers, more and more people are putting themselves at risk to go down this road. Do you think it's a coincidence that people are experiencing more problems with alcohol as well? According to the NIAAA, "The number

---

3 Yerby, Nathan. "Statistics on Addiction in America." addictioncenter.com. 5 Dec 2019. Web. 11 Dec 2019.

4 National Institute on Alcohol Abuse and Alcoholism. "Alcohol Facts and Statistics." niaaa.nih.gov. Feb 2020. Web. 11 Dec 2019.

5 Stobbe, Mike. "US drinking more now than just before Prohibition." APNews. com. The Associated Press. 14 Jan 2020. Web. 20 Jan 2020.

of death certificates mentioning alcohol more than doubled from 35,914 in 1999 to 72,558 in 2017."[6]

Those are crazy numbers and crazy trends. It's absolute brainwashing that this stuff isn't talked about the same way opioids are. I count myself truly blessed not to be a part of those statistics anymore. I consider myself lucky that I'm less likely to die of liver failure or some other horrible disease caused by my own actions. I don't want to kill myself. How about you?

The Undisclosed Shortcomings of AA

After I made my rock-bottom-escaping phone call to my boss, I didn't get sober overnight. It took about six months to really commit to the path I'm currently on. And that's because this path wasn't clear to me in the beginning. It was why it felt like I was in a lose-lose situation during my early days of trying to get sober. At the time, I thought that rehab, followed by Alcoholics Anonymous (AA) membership, was the only path to sobriety. At least that's what everyone was telling me. So I did what I was told: I went to rehab, and I went to AA.

To be honest, formalized addiction treatment was not a bad experience for me. But that's no reason to feel hopeless if it hasn't been for you. It's also why you should know that there are paths outside formalized treatment. The SoberPower Method is one of those paths.

Looking more closely, treatment didn't get me sober, nor did it change my thought processes. What it did do was give me a break. A break from the habit of picking up a drink when I was

6 National Institutes of Health. "Alcohol-related deaths increasing in the United States." nih.gov. 10 Jan 2020. Web. 20 Jan 2020.

anxious or stressed. A break from the *creepy drunk guy* routine. And a break from the lies and bullshit. Treatment gave me time to relax and detox from alcohol, so that I no longer had any *physical* withdrawal symptoms. It also gave me a much needed fresh start. It was like hitting a reset button. But it did not remove my desire to drink. Nor did it show me how great life could be without alcohol.

Treatment does different things for different people. I can't tell you how many people I watched get healthy during treatment, only to fall back off the wagon immediately upon getting home. Back to treatment they went. Like I said, rehab did not cure me of my addiction either. Because the setting is supportive and alcohol-free (unlike the real world), rehab does little to prepare you for life after treatment. That's why so many people relapse once they get out. But the brainwashing persists. We are told that you need to go to treatment to cure your addiction, so that's what we do. We are confident we will be "fixed" there and are discouraged when it doesn't happen. I imagine that if you've believed that formalized treatment could fix your addiction, you might feel pretty hopeless if it's failed you. You might even feel like *you* are the failure. Read on, and I'll show you why that's all bullshit.

Then comes the next phase of the treatment process. Once you detox from alcohol, the rehab folks force you to attend daily AA meetings. And they expect you to adopt AA's views as your own. Not only that, most of the counselors I met at rehab straight up told me that if I didn't become a member of AA, I would never quit drinking. And they rolled their eyes at me if I didn't accept this line of thinking blindly. It's as if they think we've lost our ability to think for ourselves.

For many of the people I met during treatment, this worked just fine. Because of their past addiction, some people need to be told where to go and what to do. I get that. And if you can accept the presence of a higher power and the making amends stuff as the basis for your new life, good for you. It's still a form of self-improvement and is much better than addiction. So yeah, AA isn't all bad, and it definitely does work for some people. Not only that, AA was a trailblazer in its time. A hundred years ago, people who had a problem with alcohol were shunned from society. AA helped change that. They gave alcoholics hope and support. So I don't have a problem with AA being a way to achieve sobriety, but I do have a problem with being told that it's the *only* way. In fact, AA success rates are highly questionable, and if we're being honest, AA doesn't work for most of us.

According to Zachary Dodes, author of *The Sober Truth: Debunking the Bad Science Behind 12-Step Programs and the Rehab Industry*[7], "Peer reviewed studies peg the AA success rate between five and ten percent. Only one in fifteen people who enter these programs becomes and remains sober."

To put this into perspective, imagine blindly going under the knife of a brain surgeon who only has a five to ten percent success rate. I think you'd do a little more research, right? Sorry, but I think your mission to get sober is worth more than five percent odds. I think you deserve better than that. AA retention rates are just as bad. Only ten percent of newcomers stay involved after three months, and only five percent make it a full full year. So clearly, despite my counselors' insistence that AA was a surefire way to get sober, the program is not working for most alcoholics. But if you ask me, that's not even the biggest problem with AA.

---

7 Flanagin, Jake. "The Surprising Failures of 12 Steps." theatlantic.com. The Atlantic. 25 Mar 2014. Web. 11 Dec 2019.

What Good is it to Gain the World and Lose Your Soul?

Even if you end up in the slim minority who gets sober through AA, who will you be coming out of it? If you blindly accept AA's dogma as your own, what kind of life will you lead? What will you be forced to accept? In chapter one, I confessed that when my drinking was at its worst, I could barely recognize myself. I'm guessing some of you can relate. So why should you feel the same way *after* getting sober? As I said, AA is great for people who need structure and accountability. It makes sense for those who need to be told what to do and where to go. But what if you're already a structured person at heart? What if you already have a philosophy of life, and just need a productive set of habits to make it come to life? What if you don't need a personality re-set?

If you're reading this, my guess is you and I have that in common. We both have aspirations beyond getting sober. We don't need to be preached to about what's right and what's wrong. Even if we could get sober with AA, how does it *then* help us live a more fulfilling life? People like us want more than just sobriety, right? We want more than to just show up for meetings on time and follow someone else's rituals. We define sobriety as more than just putting down a drink. We see it as a chance to become our best selves. An opportunity to develop a set of habits that leads to mental and physical wellbeing and a purposeful life. In fact, this is what we have wanted all along. It's just that our drinking got in the way.

And that is what the SoberPower Method is all about. It will get you sober *and* feeling moment-to-moment gratitude. It will get you sober *and* physically fit. It will get you sober *and* following your passions. It will help you take major steps forward in achieving self-actualization. The SoberPower Method truly is a *path* forward. You don't have to run from your past. You can own and accept everything that has happened to you and enjoy the process of turning your life around. There is no reason to be fearful. My experiences with AA led me to none of these things. You may have had a similar experience.

I'm guessing you can relate with why I couldn't accept AA into my life. I haven't been to a single meeting since my time in rehab. I want you to know that you're not "taking sobriety lightly" just because you're not interested in AA. Don't listen to the professionals and the scripted guilt trips they unleash upon you. Five to ten percent of people get sober with AA. Many more get sober without it. And I am one of those people. Before we put this topic to bed, and move on, let me officially lay out the reasons I wanted nothing to do with AA:

- With AA, you are constantly beating yourself up about the past. Sure, I've made some mistakes over the years. I'm guessing you have, too. Everyone makes mistakes, whether they drink too much or not. But AA expects us to constantly rehash and focus on our past mishaps. Sure, I owe some apologies. And we should all strive to be better people. But the last thing I want to do is live in the past. How about you? Yet, during the "share" segment of AA meetings, you commonly hear people with decades of sobriety revisit dumb drunk stories from their twenties. Who cares! Move on! I want to work on living in the present and planning for my future. How about you?

- AA claims that it's not a religious organization. Well, it sure seems like one to me. At the foundation of AA are their 12 Steps with the second one stating "[that we] came to believe that a Power greater than ourselves could restore us to sanity." Think that's a typo? The third step says, "[We] made a decision to turn our will and our lives over to the care of God as we understood Him." As an avid meditator and open-minded person, I felt like I was being force fed Sunday School material all over again. Of course, AA tells us that our "Higher Power" can be anything, even a doorknob. For real? I'm not saying I have all the answers to this life and whatever may lie beyond. But I don't think anyone in AA does either. And I'm not saying spirituality has no role in helping you achieve sobriety. On the contrary, exploring your spirituality is a vital part of the SoberPower Method. But I don't believe in praying to some repackaged version of Jesus to keep me sober. The SoberPower Method is all about empowerment, and you don't have to accept anyone's mysterious teachings to get sober.

- AA members seem to miss drinking. It's as if they've lost their dog or something. Although they are unable to forgive themselves for their past mistakes, they talk about those same times as if they were the good old days. Like they actually *miss* the thing that was ruining their lives. How screwed up is that? From my experience attending meetings and my conversations with AA members, I feel that many people in AA still wish they could drink. Many of them refer to drinkers as "normies." It's as if they wish they could be one! How sad is it to wish you could do something that you know will ruin your life? And to feel like you're missing out on one of life's great pleasures. You read the statistics at the beginning of this chapter. Bottom line, alcohol is an addictive drug that is responsible for 5.3 percent of deaths worldwide. I don't know about you, but I refuse to believe I'm "not normal" because I'm not a drug user. Honestly, once you put down your last drink, you are finally normal, and you aren't an alcoholic anymore. Pretty soon, you realize you are giving up nothing by taking on this new life. I want sobriety to be about an improved life across the board. I want to be thinking clearly and working hard in the gym. I want to be following my passions and building a positive community. I want to enjoy my life and be grateful that I finally made the decision to quit poisoning myself. That's what is normal to me now. And I sure as hell don't miss the days when all of those things weren't happening.

- Most AA members I know live in constant fear. They are afraid that they will one day give in to temptation and start drinking again. They are scared they will relapse. That's exactly why some of them keep going to meetings every week for ten, twenty, thirty years, like they're on some kind of self-imposed probation. To them, a slip-up is always right around the corner and you have to constantly be on guard against the lurking demon of alcoholism. To be fair, I agree that one drink could eventually lead me on a tailspin back into addiction. I'm a compulsive person. But I'm not fearful that it's going to happen. I'm *confident* that it will not because I have no interest in that first drink. I also believe that the longer we walk this path, the stronger we become. At this point, I barely even think about alcohol and can hardly remember what it was like to drink. Alcohol has no power over me, even in the form of fear. And the memories of my drinking days will only continue to fade with every day of sobriety. I have no reason to fear, and every reason to be confident of what may happen down the road. I'm telling you, it's amazing doing this with SoberPowers.

If you're nodding your head in agreement, it's a good thing we found each other. I'd like to propose a different and more empowering path for people like you and I. Otherwise, we're left with the same lose-lose situation I was facing while in formalized treatment:

Option #1: Keep drinking and lose everything. Get fired from my job. My family and friends desert me. End up fat, broke, and dying of an exploding kidney under a bridge.

Option #2: Join AA and spend the rest of my life mourning the past, fearing a relapse, praying for a higher power to save me, and envying normies.

Although I would gladly pick the second option over the first, this was not a crossroads I was happy to find myself at. I'm guessing you would have felt the same way. Maybe you still do. I knew there had to be another way for me. One that's more flexible and geared towards a growth mindset.

A Third Option that Changes *Everything*

As I said at the beginning of this chapter, there was a six-month gap between that rock bottom phone call to my boss and my last sip of alcohol. Change didn't happen overnight for me. During that time, I explored everything. I went to treatment and even some AA meetings. But that way of life wasn't going to work for me. I didn't give up, though. I looked for a new way. In fact, searching for a fulfilling new lifestyle became my singular mission. I woke up early, read books about sobriety, connected with others in similar situations, meditated daily, changed up my diet, and did whatever it took to break free of the drinking cycle. To find a way that *would* work for me.

Formalized treatment was a great wake-up call, but my real strides were made outside of it. Instead of blindly accepting AA dogma, attending dull meetings, and finding a sponsor to reprimand me, I looked within. I wanted to find *my* motivations for getting sober. I wanted to find a lifestyle that would keep *me* sober. I didn't just want to stop drinking. I wanted to start living an amazing life. And I wanted to truly grow as a person. It took a fair amount of time, and it wasn't always easy, but it worked. I found that third option.

Of course, this was blasphemy to the majority of my counselors at treatment. They prophesied an early relapse for me and a "tail between my legs" trip back to the clinic. Maybe that's what they wanted. I wish I could say they were at least respectful in giving their opinions on how I should live my life. My friends from treatment still scoff when I tell them that I don't have a sponsor to confess my sins to. If you've been evangelized by AA, my guess is, you can relate. One last issue I have with AA is its black-and-white approach to everything. This affects how it treats potential members as well. With AA, you are either with them or you are not. And they don't have very nice things to say about people like me who don't jump aboard the bandwagon.

The third option that I found doesn't have time for that kind of judgement, nor does it have time for rules and punishment. It's open, forgiving, and personal. And it puts *you* at the center of *your* new life. As you probably have gathered by now, the third option is called the SoberPower Method. It was the answer to my "lose-lose situation" and the lifestyle I was looking for.

So what's the SoberPower Method all about and what can you expect from it? Good question. With the SoberPower Method:

- Your sober journey will be a meaningful and enjoyable experience from day one. The process is all about building healthy habits. Although acquiring new habits is challenging at first, it's not some terrible ordeal you have to go through in order to earn a token. There are no steps, sponsors, or regrets. You will actually enjoy getting your SoberPowers.

- You will truly be free from alcohol. And you won't have to refer to yourself as an alcoholic for the rest of your life. In fact, alcohol will have no power over you whatsoever. You will learn that you are giving up nothing when you get sober, and you won't envy the normies who still *have* to drink.

- You will be living your best life and growing in every possible way. You will not be merely getting sober, and you will not be living in the past. You will be getting mentally and physically healthier than you've ever been. And you will lay the groundwork for a truly purposeful life.

Sounds better than bad coffee in a church basement, right?

One thing I did know was that choosing this path would be the most defining moment of my life. If you have higher ambitions than to spend the rest of your life crawling around and begging for forgiveness, you're going to love the SoberPower Method. For the past two years, I have listened to my heart and taken action. And I have found a way to cut ties with my past life and bad habits. I found the path to new habits—habits that would not only get me

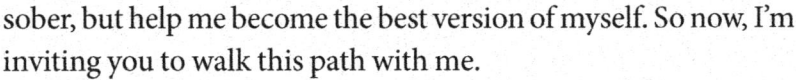

sober, but help me become the best version of myself. So now, I'm inviting you to walk this path with me.

CHAPTER 3

FINDING YOUR SOBERPOWERS

"So, if desire cannot be turned off or seduced away from addictive goals, immediate goals, then it has to be fastened to goals incompatible with addiction—goals such as freedom from suffering, achievement of life projects, access to loving relationships, and the sense of coherence and self-love that can come with abstinence . . . Desire has the power to propel us through life, to get us from now to later." (Marc Lewis, The Biology of Desire)

During my stint in treatment, I found out that a narrow-minded approach to sobriety would not work for me. I also realized that getting back to some semblance of normality would not be enough. I wanted more. I experimented with anything and everything, and that's how I found the SoberPower Method. With it, I have been sober for over two years and rarely even think about drinking. I don't refer to myself as an alcoholic, because those days are long gone. During my two years of sobriety, I've grown mentally, physically, and spiritually in ways I never thought possible. My life is better now than it ever has been. I'm truly free.

The SoberPower Mentality

The SoberPower Method is simple and straightforward. It doesn't treat you like some miserable person because you aren't allowed to drink anymore like the normies. By following the SoberPower Method, you will lose all desire to drink and therefore be free of all cravings in the long run. You won't be the *creepy sober guy* at the party who is drinking sparkling water and envying your friends either. Instead, you'll be the sober one in the group, and a beacon of light to all your friends and colleagues. You won't envy them one bit. Unlike most drinkers, you will have natural confidence and won't need to drink to have a good time. You will be authentically yourself at all times. You will look and feel better than anyone else because you will have a healthy lifestyle. You'll sleep great. You'll never be hungover. You'll do better in your career because you'll actually have the time and energy to make things happen. You'll maintain the best relationships you've ever had because you'll no longer settle for anything (or anyone) less than you deserve. You'll be confident and in control. You'll be firing on all cylinders, instead of living as a shadow of yourself.

Having SoberPowers will also change the way other people see and treat you. Some will actually envy you because you'll be doing what seems impossible to them. Since I've stopped drinking, I can't count how many times I've overheard people saying they wish they drank less alcohol or that they were going dry for a week to detox. You know, all the Dry January crap. How amazing it is to be out of this terrible cycle of alcohol addiction! Even people who aren't necessarily problem drinkers know they should, and wish they could, cut back. When you have SoberPowers, you'll be the one actually *doing* it. In no way will you be handicapped or deserving of sympathy. In fact, you'll be operating on a higher level than anyone in the room. If you think any of this sounds overstated, just keep reading . . .

SoberPowered vs "Recovered" Alcoholic

Being someone with SoberPowers is a far cry from being your typical AA member. More often than not, AA members avoid going out. In fact, they avoid any situation in which alcohol is present. I reluctantly went to a few AA meetings during my time in treatment, but didn't run into many people who were in good shape. Many of them complain about compulsive eating. They don't have much to say about their awesome life without alcohol and all the new habits and goals they are working towards. They prefer to talk about that DUI from '97. And worse, even the most successful members talk and act as if they feel sorry for themselves. As if they made some horrible mistake, one that will take a lifetime to "recover" from. I couldn't agree to that life two years ago, and I can't do it now. I mean, how can you call yourself "recovered," and yet describe yourself as someone who *still* has the disease? It just doesn't make sense.

I'd also add that my sobriety defies a fundamental assumption that AA practically treats as religious dogma. Meaning, if I haven't attended 12-step meetings, like seemingly every other person in recovery, how have I gone two years without craving a single drink? The answer is the SoberPower Method.

The SoberPower Method does not include negativity. With AA, you are led to believe that you are sick and that you always will be an alcoholic. You are given a life sentence. But who came up with that diagnosis? It just doesn't compute for me. Once you stop drinking, you are not sick anymore, because it's the alcohol that made you sick in the first place. I'm living proof of that. I'm in better shape than just about anyone I know. I feel amazing spiritually and mentally. I have tons of energy throughout the day to work on projects and relationships. I have no cravings or desires to drink or go back to my old ways. So how am I still an alcoholic? In what way am I sick? In short, I feel great and see no reason to stray from this path—ever. This is the life I desire, and I wake up every day fired up to live it. There is no fear of going back to drinking, because not a single part of me wishes to do so. To me, that sounds better than spending the next 30 years saying, "Hi, my name is Drew, and I'm an alcoholic."

To move on with your life and be free from alcohol, you have to have a positive attitude about choosing sobriety. Sure, say sorry to those that you hurt. Spend some time making amends. But then move on! This is the start of something great, and it will undoubtedly be the best decision of your life. Remember that, starting today, you will have the time and energy to create the life you always dreamed of. That nagging alcohol addiction that was holding you back will finally be gone. You won't be sick, in recovery, or worth any less than your friends. On the contrary, you'll be in a better spot than even the lightest of drinkers. You will never have another hangover for the rest of your life. For the past two years, I've woken up every morning feeling rested and energized. And I cannot stress enough just how amazing of an improvement that is. I'm not sick anymore. The nightmare is over!

However, removing constant hangovers from your life is only the beginning. The SoberPower Method takes you beyond sobriety from drinking and into consistent growth in all areas of your life. You will become stronger mentally, physically, *and* spiritually. In fact, I can tell you that the past two years have hardly seemed like recovery to me. This is more about living the good life, and things will only get better as we keep improving ourselves.

"Alright, that's enough. So what the hell is the SoberPower Method?" Ok, I hear you and can see that I'm rambling a bit. I'm just that fired up. Here you go.

The SoberPower Method: A Six-Part SoberPractice

The SoberPower Method is all about establishing healthy habits that improve your life. Taken together, these habits will form your SoberPractice. There are six parts to the SoberPractice, each addressing a critical area of building an amazing sober life. Each one is important alone, but together, they will get you sober and on a meaningful path forward. Your SoberPractice will not just help you get sober. It will make your sobriety worth it. Here is a brief overview of the SoberPractice. We will go into each part, in detail, later in the book.

Part #1: Commit

The first part of the SoberPractice is a bit different than the others. The other five parts are all about building healthy habits in the most important areas of your life. But in order to build habits, you have to be willing to work. And in order to have the discipline to work, you have to be motivated. And in order to be motivated, you have to be committed. So the first part of the SoberPractice isn't a habit. It's a set of commitments that kicks off the whole process.

The first commitment is to be sober. It's simply impossible to work your SoberPractice while maintaining any semblance of your previous lifestyle. The second commitment is to prioritize your SoberPractice. You have to carve out some time to put yourself, and your habits, first. Once you commit, you are ready to go.

Part #2: Learn

As I said before, our society is brainwashed to believe that drinking is a good thing and that it's hard to quit. It paints sober people as sick and in need of daily recovery. And even if they succeed, after all of that recovery work, they are at best social outcasts who have given up their chance of being normal. This was how I felt after I quit drinking, and it scared the crap out of me. I wasn't about to spend the rest of my evenings in church basements while my friends got to keep living it up. I wanted to see if there was a better way to live. There is. *Learning the truth about alcohol was my ticket to an improved mindset and lifestyle.*

While addicted and trying to get sober, I was brainwashed. I didn't know what to believe. So I started my sober journey by reading a bunch of books written by people who had been where I had been and who had succeeded in getting sober. I read everything to get different perspectives about how to quit drinking. The most important book I found was *Kick the Drink . . . Easily* by Jason Vale. I can honestly credit this book as the most significant thing I've found in my journey to sobriety. Vale's perspective was completely new to me, and it changed my life. The book is designed to speak to your subconscious, so that you can remove all the dangerous pro-alcohol brainwashing you've been exposed to. I talked earlier about how dangerous those thoughts are. It's a big reason we got into this mess. *Kick the Drink* teaches you that by quitting drinking, you are giving up nothing. Rather, you are finally getting your life back and making the smart choice to stop consuming the most abused poison in the world. Vale reminds us that the second we put our last drink down, we are free. I was fired up to be a sober person after I read this book, and that feeling has not gone away in the two years since. This is why I consider reading *Kick the Drink* as a major step of the SoberPractice.

Pretty soon, your entire attitude towards sobriety will change. You will start to see how lucky you are to be in your position. Your subconscious mind will shift, and you will know the truth of both alcohol and sobriety. You will be smarter and more confident. And that's just the start.

After reading *Kick the Drink* for a few weeks, I no longer felt depressed and scared about moving on from alcohol. Instead, I felt relieved that I was quitting. I no longer envied people who were still drinking. I felt grateful to be among the few who could see through the brainwashing and lies. I felt grateful to be alive and hopeful for the future.

Part #3: Sweat

So now you're getting smarter. And you're beginning to see sobriety in a positive light. So what do you do next? For me, the next step was becoming physically healthy as well. As a drinker, I was overweight and had low levels of energy. Quite simply, this was because I was addicted to a poison, ate unhealthy foods, and was too anxious to get quality sleep. Now that this drug is removed from my life, I want to make the most of the time I have left on this planet. So improving my body was the next focus of my sober journey. And it is the next step of the SoberPractice.

Getting fit is pretty damn simple actually. All you have to do his exercise consistently, eat healthy foods, and get adequate sleep. Boom, that's it. I will go into each of these areas specifically in the coming chapters. For now, just note that once you have these three bases covered, you will have positive energy throughout the day.

You will also release a shit ton of endorphins that will literally make you happier. There are no gimmicks or tricks here. This is basic stuff. You will lose that beer belly and turn your sick body into a healthy one. And you will feel great doing it. You will start to look like a new person after a few short weeks, and your attitude and lifestyle will follow suit.

One additional benefit of getting your body healthy is that it creates massive amounts of positive reinforcement. This is important as it's vital that you recognize the decision to quit drinking as a positive one. You want to associate being sober with being healthy, present, and disciplined. Getting fit is one of the best ways to do this, as the results are obvious and visible. When you look in the mirror and see your skin and body improving, it will be very hard to convince yourself to go back to your old ways of drinking.

Part #4: Sit

The fourth part of the SoberPractice is to learn to feel gratitude and acceptance. Oh, and I don't mean saying "thanks" to your waiter. It's much deeper than that. There's a dramatic difference between expressing gratitude and feeling it down in your gut. In my opinion, it's the building block of a healthy spiritual life. The first thing you need is to *find some alone time and sit down.* Stillness is your friend here. Are you sitting? Good. What happens next is up to you.

If you're new to this, a few minutes of journaling everyday should do the trick. Start by writing down one thing you're grateful for every morning. If you are already an experienced meditator, your practice can bring forth feelings of gratitude as well. Prayer works too. It all depends on your background and style. The main thing to note is that we need to find gratitude for the present moment and acceptance of our current self. That way, you won't just be smarter regarding your alcohol addiction. Your emotional and spiritual life will get back on track as well. You will no longer be a slave to your feelings. You will be making smart decisions because you'll be working from a position of gratitude and abundance. But it all starts by turning off your phone, finding a quiet place, and sitting down.

Why is gratitude the goal? Because it's the only thing that can raise you out of the states of fear, scarcity, and competitiveness. When we operate in one of these three toxic states, we infect ourselves with the belief there isn't enough good (i.e., love, money, opportunity) to go around. We live in fear that we have to get something before someone else "beats us to it," or that the good things in our life will eventually abandon us. Going further, these negative states bring on the belief that we are not enough, and that we don't have enough to be happy at this very moment. Thoughts like these were undoubtedly at the center of our addiction. Even in sobriety, this is a horrible way to live, and can turn a decent person into an angry and self-centered shadow of themselves. But gratitude lifts you out of these states by turning your attention to the good that's already in your life. It moves you out of the realm of mere survival and into the realm of possibility. Gratitude shows you that you have everything you need, right now, to be happy. Take a seat.

Part #5: Connect

At this point, you'll be seeing past all the pro-alcohol brainwashing handed down to you by society. You'll be excited to be a sober person, and you'll be feeling gratitude for being alive. You'll also have a healthy lifestyle, getting plenty of sleep, and hitting the gym. Your body will feel great, and you'll have consistent energy throughout the day. But we can't do this alone, right? The fifth part of the SoberPractice is all about connecting with the right people.

As a drinker, you most likely spend a lot of time with negative people who do not really care about you. I've been there, and it sucks. Think about all the times in your life when you have been depressed. Isn't it usually because of something wrong with one of your relationships? Think about the times you have been anxious. Didn't this often have to do with how you felt you were being viewed by others? Bottom line, relationships matter. They form the core of our emotional lives. Being around great people and fostering amazing relationships with them will solve the majority of your emotional problems. So now it's time to build a positive social circle.

I know this is contrary to what you might have read in other self-help books. They tell you things like "you have to love yourself before anyone else can love you." In a way, I understand why they'd say that. But people who write this also neglect the powerful influence of your social circle. The idea that you have to get well before you can attract good relationships also traps you in a cycle of "trying to be good enough." But as you follow the SoberPower Method, you'll realize that changing your relationships is just as important as changing yourself.

You've probably done quite a bit of relationship damage during your drinking years. Make it a point to fix what you can, and then build a solid social foundation for yourself. These people will help you pull through anything, so that all your future challenges will be that much easier. And you will do the same for them, establishing a positive feedback loop that will change your life. It's time to show the world the new sober version of yourself.

By connecting with others, the fifth part of the SoberPractice helps to make that happen

Part #6: Hustle

At this point, you will be healthier and happier than you ever were as a drinker. You'll have no regrets. And you'll have some good people by your side that you connect with on the regular. But you aren't done. Now it's time to think big picture. What are your goals in life, and how are you going to get there? How can you make an impact on the world and leave a legacy you will be proud of? Yeah, I went there. Up until now, you've mainly been focused on yourself. Don't get me wrong, improving yourself is one of the best gifts you can give to others. But now it's time to turn your attention outward. The sixth, and final, part of the SoberPractice is all about the hustle. It's about finding your purpose and doing meaningful work that you are passionate about.

If you're anything like I was, you've probably been coasting through your career without clear goals. If you're a heavy drinker, it's hard to do much else. I know that I hated to live like that. The good news is that we are going to change all that. We are going to be productive again. We are going to work harder on better projects. We are going to live with intention and make the world a better place. If this sounds overwhelming right now, don't worry. Once you have all the previous SoberPractice steps aligned, you'll be eager to get started in this final area.

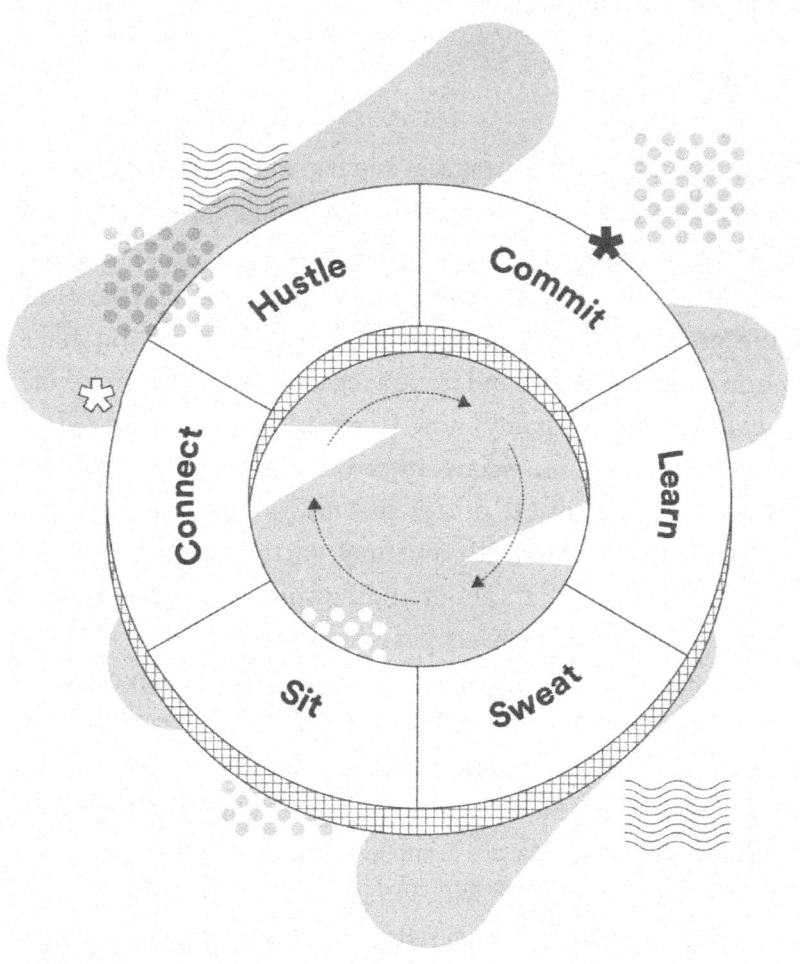

With your improved social circle and newfound healthy habits by your side, you can finally start to figure out what you want to do with your life. As a drinker, I put this off forever. Now, I like to call this my ultimate purpose, mission, or most important work. Whatever you want to call it, this newfound purpose will get you out of bed, excited and energized, for the day ahead. It's your *it*, and you discover what your *it* is by making time each day to follow your passions. You will find your *it* at the intersection of what you are good at, what you enjoy doing, and what you can do for other people.

Even if this seems impossible right now, it will feel totally natural once you get to this part of your SoberPractice. Answering these questions will make your new life more than just a sober existence. It will make every day meaningful as you start your journey towards true self-actualization. And it will allow you to make the world a better place—something I believe we were all put here to do. Again, SoberPowers aren't just for getting sober. They're for making your life amazing, so that you'll never want to make yourself sick again

So now you have an idea of what my third option, and alternative to AA, is. It's a SoberPractice that is built up over time through new habit formation.

Together, these six parts form your SoberPractice, which is the core work of the SoberPower Method. It's what you do every day to transform out of being an addicted person in a crappy life situation into someone operating at a high level with SoberPowers. Your SoberPractice is what you are fired up to do every day. We'll unpack each part in the coming chapters to help you get started. We will also give you an idea of how to implement this into your day, so that you are not overwhelmed. With the SoberPower Method, our focus is consistency over intensity.

You Are Your Habits

Quitting drinking is not complicated, and it's not some terrible ordeal you have to go through. It has been the best experience of my life, and it can be for you as well. Learning the truth about alcohol taught me that I wouldn't have to give up anything when I put down the booze. Instead, I gave myself the health, time, and energy to go after the things I really want in life. I'm still on that path and would never go back to the stressful days of drinking. With the SoberPower Method, you'll be focusing less on strict goals and timelines, and more on habits and growth. This is why there are no 30-day chips with the SoberPower Method. There is no waiting. Just the commitment to change and the discipline to re-create your habits.

Let me finish this chapter by saying that this may seem like a lot to do, and you've probably been drinking for many years. Like I was, you are set in your ways and drinking has become a habit for you. All of the sections of the SoberPractice, described above, may seem overwhelming. Well, I agree that it is a lot of work. But it's work that you need to be doing anyway in order to say "yes" to a healthy and successful life. Sober or not, you need to be getting good sleep in order to have consistent energy. Drinker or not, you should be building a solid social network for yourself. Similar things could be said about anything on this list. So this isn't really adding much onto the most widely accepted habits used for success and wellness. And the only difference is now you have more time to put 100% effort into this. You will have much more energy to build a great SoberPractice that improves you in all areas.

And as someone with a drinking habit who struggles to even get up for the day, it may seem like a lot to keep track of. True, it will until this lifestyle becomes your new habit. As such, the steps of your SoberPractice will become positive habits that replace the habit of drinking. This is why the SoberPower Method is about more than just sobriety. It's a way of life that you can feel passionate about, and it's a set of habits that are incompatible with further drinking. So you can quit drinking and build a great life all at once. It won't be easy in the beginning, as old habits are hard to break, but I can tell you that it will be worth it.

CHAPTER 4

ALL ABOUT HABITS

"Most of the recovered addicts I've talked to would rather think of themselves as free—not cured, not in remission. Having overcome their addictions by dint of hard work, intense self-examination, and the courage and capacity to regrow their perspectives (and their synapses), they'd rather see themselves as having developed through addiction and become stronger as a result." (Marc Lewis, The Biology of Desire)

The SoberPower Method has been an absolute game changer for me. It has kept me sober, while pushing me to grow mentally, physically, and spiritually. It has added so much meaning to my life and changed things in ways I never before thought possible. And if I'm being honest, it's been the best time of my life. That said, it didn't click for me overnight, and it may not for you either. It takes time in the beginning because your SoberPractice is all about building and maintaining healthy habits. We all know that old habits can be hard to break just as new ones can be difficult to form. There are two factors that will work in your favor here:

1) A strong desire to be sober and to find a new way of life.

2) The discipline to push through initial friction during the habit loading phase.

If you are hooked on drinking, and looking to quit, you must want sobriety more than anything else. More importantly, you must desire a new way of life. One that doesn't include drinking. In other words, you have to want to pursue a healthy lifestyle *more* than you want to drink. You need to truly love it and be willing to work for it. I shared with you some of the benefits I experienced while getting my SoberPowers. Don't you want the same for yourself? You need to envision what your life will be like in three months, a year, and ten years. Who will you be surrounded by? What will you create? With the SoberPower Method, this is all possible as your life will improve by leaps and bounds.

Outside of sheer desire, you also need to have the discipline and mental focus to get started. Creating new habits is not easy. But once established, they are strong and difficult to break. That's why with the SoberPower Method, the most challenging work takes place on the front end. It's also the most exhilarating time as you get to see how much opportunity lies in front of you. For many people, the most difficult thing is having the right set of habits that lead to happiness. If you are anything like I used to be, your drinking habit has not been doing this for you. It's time to turn that around. The six parts of the SoberPractice are your cheat sheet.

Habits are simple. Our brains create habits automatically to serve as shortcuts to get us from point A to point B. Like brushing your teeth in the morning, habits can be easy and effective. They can take the thinking out of normal, everyday actions. But what if point A isn't all that great? And what if point B isn't much better? Habits can also be self-destructive. My point A was stressful life situations, and my point B was a rock bottom brought on by heavy drinking. I needed to turn this around. I needed my habits to work for me, and not against me. I needed a new point B, so I needed new habits to take me there.

The Habit Loading Phase

Building these habits required discipline, in the beginning, when my habit of drinking was still in play. Things got much easier, though. After a few months of hard work, I had a new set of habits and was well on my way to a new point B. I was thrust out of rock bottom and into the land of opportunity. And because these new habits were established as routine, the level of required discipline dropped off substantially.[8]

I know I keep saying it, but the SoberPower Method is simple and enjoyable. And once your SoberPractice becomes a habit, it's also quite easy. But it will take some focused effort to get started. I know that the thought of never drinking again is daunting, and simultaneously working on all the major aspects of yourself can seem intimidating. That's why we are going to take this slow and focus on the present moment.

The next five months will be your *habit loading phase*. When you use discipline to turn the habit of drinking into the habit of working your SoberPractice. During this time, your brain will change. Scientists call this phenomenon "neuroplasticity." What this means for you is that the old and ineffective neural pathways

8 Tynan. *Superhuman by Habit: A Guide to Becoming the Best Possible Version of Yourself, One Tiny Habit at a Time.* Amazon.com Services LLC, 2014.

that kept you reaching for a drink will lose their strength. At the same time, you will also create new pathways that lead to new habits. The habits of your SoberPractice will lead to you having SoberPowers. Five months is all it takes to get on this path. So what do you do during this five month habit loading phase? Here's how it works.

Your SoberPractice consists of the six parts described in the previous chapter: Commit, Learn, Sweat, Sit, Connect, and Hustle. The first part, Commit, is a little different as it happens the day you put down this book. It's a decision. It's instantaneous and a clean cut from your previous life of drinking. The other five parts take a bit more time as they involve habit loading. You will focus on one habit per month, and add the other parts incrementally. The thinking here is that it takes about a month to fully load a habit. A month to re-wire your brain. At that point, you will have that specific habit automated and you can move onto the next one. That doesn't mean you stop the habits you've acquired during the previous month. It just means that they are automatic, and you no longer have to think about them as much. So you can focus on the next area of self-improvement.

Here's the five month plan:

- Day 1: Commit

- Month 1: Learn

- Month 2: Sweat

- Month 3: Sit

- Month 4: Connect

- Month 5: Hustle

To give a point in time example, during the third month, you'll have already Committed to sobriety and ingrained the Learn and Sweat habits. Now, you are focusing on the Sit habits like it's your job. And you aren't even thinking about the Connect and Hustle areas of your SoberPractice. You aren't worrying about them. You are only worried about the Sit area as everything else is either fully ingrained or reserved for a future month.

Given this cadence, it will take about five months to turn every aspect of your SoberPractice into regular routine and habit. Keep in mind that this is the most challenging time, but also the most rewarding. If you can get through this period, you'll have some solid sober time under your belt, positive feedback, and a break from the struggle. More importantly, the hard work and discipline will pay off as your SoberPractice becomes an established habit. You'll have your *own* SoberPowers.

During these five months, your SoberPractice will be the number one priority in your life. You will attack self-improvement from all angles. You also won't be drinking. Five months may seem like a long time to not drink, but my hope is that you will enjoy the process of improving yourself and will not want to mess that up with alcohol. Like I said, for people like us, drinking and self-improvement are mutually exclusive. Moderation may work for some things, but not when you're poisoning yourself.

It is my personal experience that the next five months will go a long way to getting you back on track. More than that, this journey will show you what is possible for the rest of your life if you put down the nasty habit of drinking and focus on acquiring healthy habits. You will slowly, but consistently, become the best version of yourself, and you will see this unfold every day. Seeing yourself grow and progress will make your decision to be sober easier with each new day. That's the goal of the SoberPower

Method: to make your life so fulfilling, after five months, that you will have zero interest in going back to your old ways. You are about to get all aspects of your life on track, and it will feel amazing. There is zero chance of this happening if you continue to drink, even just a little bit.

Lastly, I want to stress how important it is that the six parts of your SoberPractice are worked on in the correct order. Truly, a sick mind cannot sustain a healthy body for long, nor can an unhealthy person give 100 percent effort to their most important work. This is why the SoberPower Method focuses on building these habits, slowly and incrementally, in the above order. I can't wait for you to see all the progress you'll make.

One Important Disclaimer

Here's the thing. I don't believe that I, or anybody else, know you like you do. It is not my goal to tell you how to live your life. I'll leave that to the folks at AA. You have to listen to your own heart and embark on your own journey. That said, you are currently an addicted person who is most likely unsure of himself. You haven't been taking care of yourself, and your habits could use some improvement. Your subconscious is also under the influence of a culture that believes alcohol is a positive thing. For this reason, I'm asking you to trust me for the next five months only. Follow the SoberPower Method with an open mind during this time, so that you can get out of your rut and start your new sober life. The habits you build are based on universal principles of health and happiness (i.e., exercise). Once you've made it through the next five months, you'll be sober, healthy, and filled with gratitude. At this point, you can continue to follow the same SoberPractice, as

I have done, or you can build your own practice based on your newfound perspective and momentum.

Five months is all I ask. Do this, and see for yourself where the SoberPower Method will take you. You will certainly hear no objections from me if you feel like this hasn't worked out for you by then. If, after five months, you are still wanting to drink and not be the best version of yourself, feel free to try a different approach. I can promise you—AA and rehab clinics will not be closing their doors anytime soon. At the very minimum, you can say that you didn't have a drink for five months, which is a pretty big accomplishment in and of itself.

After five months, the hardest parts of achieving sobriety and acquiring SoberPowers are over. You will have gotten through the habit loading phase for each of the six areas, and you will have a new set of healthy habits that will have you on a meaningful path. From a habit building perspective, you will enter the *maintenance phase*. At this point, you will be more relaxed and thinking clearly, as the discipline required to maintain your habits drops off. Like me, you may even get to the point where you don't think about sobriety all that much. That's how building habits works. Once you have them, all it takes is a little bit of work to maintain them for life. That's the theory behind the SoberPower Method. Things get easier over time as the effects and momentum from your habits solidifies.

The funny thing is, I actually miss the old days during my own habit loading phase. Starting out on all of this was an amazing part of my journey. I was so singularly focused. It is my hope that you find the next five months to be some of the best of your life. If you decide to stick with this long term, the changes made will be a sign of many good things to come. As I keep saying, I believe five months is enough time to establish some habits. It's enough time to make some progress. It's enough time to see things a bit differently and experience a shift in mindset. As a habitual drinker, you more than likely need all of these things.

For the next several chapters, we're going to dig into each of the six parts of the SoberPractice, and we'll talk about the benefits of each and every habit. After that, you will be ready to start your own SoberPractice. And you'll be well on your way to finding your own SoberPowers.

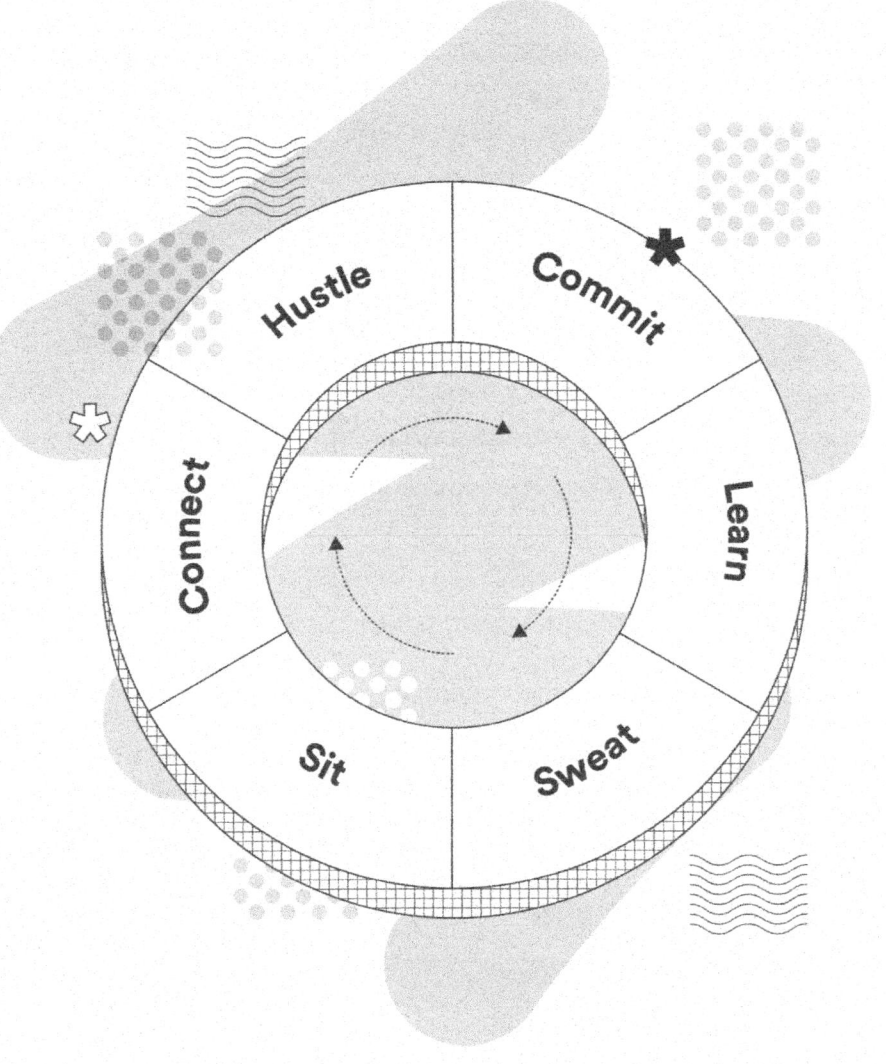

CHAPTER 5

COMMIT

═══════════════════════════════════

"Until one is committed, there is hesitancy, the chance to draw back, always ineffectiveness. Concerning all acts of initiative (and creation) there is one elementary truth, the ignorance of which kills countless ideas and splendid plans: that the moment that one definitely commits oneself, then Providence moves too. All sorts of things occur to help one that would never otherwise have occurred. A whole stream of events issues from the decision, raising in one's favor all manner of unforeseen incidents and meetings and material assistance, which no man could have dreamed could have come his way." (John Dupuy, Integral Recovery)[9]

The first step of the SoberPractice is simple and maybe obvious. And you'll do it on day one when you put down this book. It's even included in the name of the program. The first thing you must do to embark on this journey and gain your SoberPowers

---

9 Dupay, John. *Integral Recovery: A Revolutionary Approach to the Treatment of Alcoholism and Addiction.* Excelsior Editions, 2013.

is . . . to actually be sober. You have to make the cold, hard decision to not pick up a drink during the next five months. *You have to commit.* In fact, that is probably why you picked up this book to begin with. But going further, it is also the only way to make the rest of the SoberPractice habits actually stick. You won't get much out of this process if you are still drinking. And you won't enjoy it either.

But outside of committing to sobriety, you have to commit to work on your SoberPractice. Every day. So promise yourself that you'll be sober, open, and focused during the next five months. This may take a bit of willpower at first. You may even have some cravings as the habit of drinking is still in play for you. I know that I did. But once you start seeing past the brainwashing and lies, your cravings will diminish rapidly. I know this from experience, and it is a core aspect of the entire SoberPower Method. But you have to commit before it gets any easier. So relax, and get ready to make the choice of sobriety with confidence. Do this knowing that things will get much better as you move forward. And remember that you are giving up nothing when you decide to quit drinking.

So now, you are sober and ready to work on all the various parts of your SoberPractice. And I know what you are thinking. You are busy. You have a job to do and kids to raise. I get it. But how good are you at your job if you're drinking all the time? And how are your kids handling your drinking problem? Truly, working on your SoberPractice needs to be your #1 priority in life right now. So you need to set aside time for it. I'd recommend first thing in the morning.

No More Wasted Time

Mornings used to be the worst time of the day for me. During my drinking days, I regularly woke up with massive anxiety, a puffy face, and a stomach ache. Usually, my first thought of the day was, "How do I survive the next 24 hours without getting caught?" Then, I would lie in bed until the last possible second before stumbling my way into another hungover day. What a winner, right? I had zero productive morning routines. I felt very little gratitude for being alive. It was a nightmare, and I don't even recognize the person I was back then.

One of the craziest things I've found since getting sober is that I'm actually a morning person. But I don't just wake up early for the hell of it. I use my high level of energy and focus to jump into my SoberPractice for the day. It's become a positive loop for me. If I maintain a healthy diet and have the rest of my SoberPractice aligned, I sleep great and wake up excited for the day ahead. That motivates me to get up early and do it all over again. And so on and so forth. This positive momentum has continued for two years. Unlike my drinking days, mornings are now the time I feel my best. It's my time to shine.

You absolutely need to set aside time for your SoberPractice. You can't compromise here. You have to learn to put yourself first. Carve out one hour of your day to be alone and building healthy habits. As a newly proclaimed morning person, I think getting up before work is the best time for this. Nobody will be texting you at that hour, and nothing else will be demanding your time. If you're like me, you may find that your energy level is highest in the morning, especially now that alcohol is out of your life. But all that said, I get it—not everybody is a morning person. And some of you may have other constraints that make mornings difficult.

Not a big deal. The most important thing is to dedicate an hour each day to work on yourself. Carve out an hour, shut out all interruptions, commit to your SoberPractice, and your life will change.

The First Hour

Here's the bonus with all of this. Even if I removed all of the SoberPractice work from my mornings, it would still be worth it to have an unstructured hour to reflect and enjoy sobriety. Seriously, just waking up early and not being hungover feels amazing. Dedicating time for my own self-improvement is empowering in and of itself. It's saying *yes* to our new sober life. It's what makes us different in the best possible way. Two years ago, when I started all this, it was the first time in years that I actually sat quietly and listened to my heart. Now, I cannot imagine what life would be like without my quiet mornings.

A wise man once said that if you make the first hour of your day great, the rest will follow automatically. In my experience, newly sober people will cherish these moments. And this will go a long way in keeping this lifestyle going. You will feel ecstatic when you get out of bed early and see how different your life is as a sober person. Similarly, you will be proud when you turn down the happy hour drinks in the afternoon so that you can work on your SoberPractice. Sure, some people will be disappointed that you're not "hanging out" anymore. This is all about putting your own wellbeing first. Addicted people don't do this. Getting your priorities straight is proof that you are in control of your life, and it will build daily positive momentum to fuel your SoberPowers.

Another benefit of dedicating an hour to your SoberPractice is that it guarantees the work will actually get done. If you aren't specific about when you do the work, you are much more likely to procrastinate, or skip it entirely. That's how it would be for me at least. Having a set time each day to work on myself makes it much more likely to actually happen. And we need our SoberPractice to happen. Truly, if you follow through with your SoberPractice, the rest of your life will fall into place. You will level up in all the key areas of wellness and have exponentially more energy than before.

During the next five months, your SoberPractice should be the most important thing in your life. It will be about more than just getting sober. It will be about moving forward with your life in the best possible way. Not to diminish the rest of your responsibilities, but once you've completed your SoberPractice, you can relax because you've handled the most meaningful part of your day. And if you are like me, you will find out that the rest of your work and responsibilities are that much easier when you are healthy and energized. When you know you've taken care of yourself, you can take it easy knowing that you are stronger than ever before and not at the mercy of alcohol. All that's left is to take action. Carve out one hour per day for your SoberPractice, and you are one step closer to having SoberPowers.

One last note on timing. The SoberPower Method will be much more enjoyable if you make it your own. For example, not all of the SoberPractice has to be done in the morning. For example, I go to the gym during my lunch break at work. So that part of my SoberPractice happens in the afternoon. And since the whole idea behind the dedicated morning hour is to have some time for yourself, you might want to connect with other people during a different time of the day. That said, use your mornings to get a good chunk of your SoberPractice done and to build positive momentum for the rest of your day. By prioritizing *some* of the work early, you will have a much better chance of getting it *all* done.

Major Commitments

So let's summarize a bit here. The first part of your SoberPractice is to Commit. You do this on day one, and you are committing to two basic things.

First, you need to commit to not drinking alcohol. As you know by now, one of the major goals of the SoberPower Method is to actually get sober. And the rest of the objectives require a sober mind. So drinking is not an option. Take a break from drinking, and begin your SoberPractice with an open mind. It will be changing and improving every day.

Your second commitment is to set aside an hour of your day to focus on your SoberPractice. Yes, everyday. I like to call this time my power hour, but I fully admit that I am a cheesy person. Regardless, it's the most important time of my day. I think the best time to work on yourself is in the morning before normal responsibilities (and your kids) beckon. However, if the morning will not work for you, find some time after work or before bed to carve out that hour. Turn off your electronic devices. Sit in a comfortable chair. Make a pot of tea. And start working on your Sober Practice. That's the second promise you are making to yourself.

Your work during this hour will consist of building the simple habits within each of the areas summarized in the previous chapter: Learn, Sweat, Sit, Connect, and Hustle. We will take it slow. You will focus on Learning the truth about alcohol and overcoming your brainwashing during the first month. Starting the second month, you will start working out. And so on and so forth. All of this is additive, so that you can take your time building each habit before moving on to the next. We will go over the details of each habit in the coming chapters.

By now, I'm sure you realize that this is not just about quitting drinking. The SoberPower Method is about becoming an empowered person. It's not enough to simply stop drinking. Quitting any persistent habit will always leave a hole in your life. This will lead to boredom, and possibly even jealousy of other people, as you just sit around the house unproductive and unmotivated. After all, at least the normies get to party while they're being unproductive! You have to fill this hole in your life by moving forward. Committing to this way of life is the first step in making that happen.

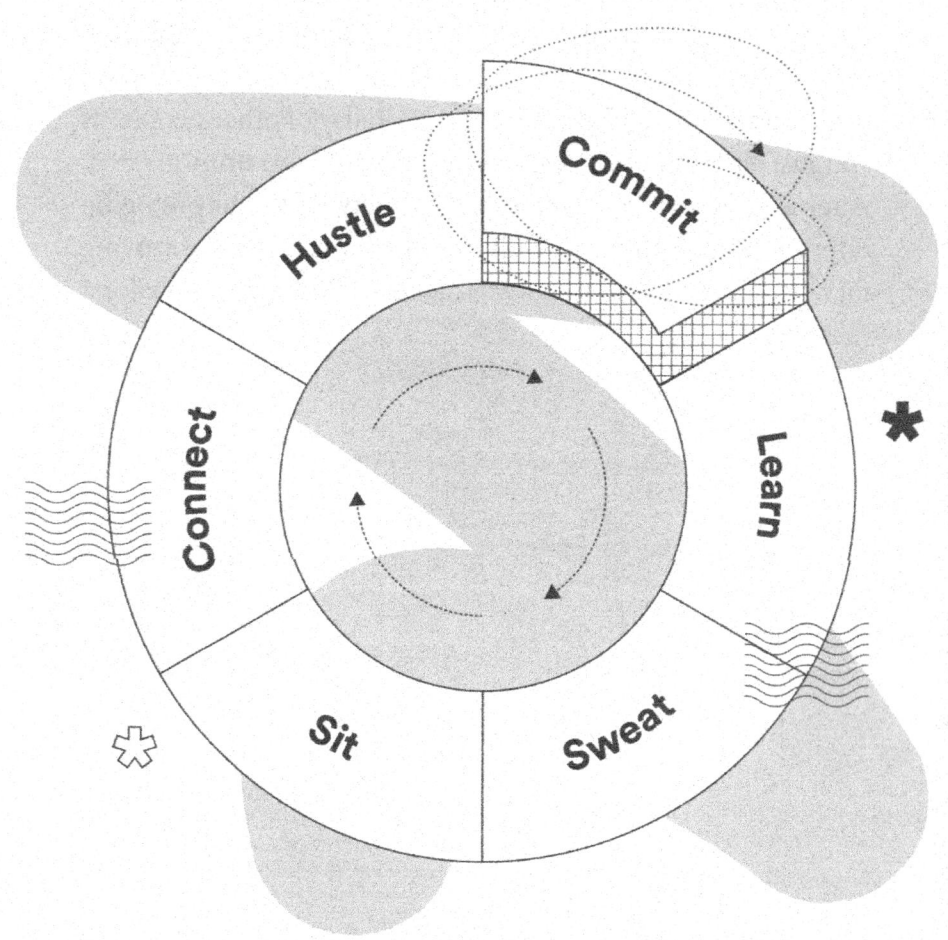

Day 1:
Commit
Commit to sobriety and
your daily SoberPractice.

CHAPTER 6

LEARN

=======================================

"If you have no desire to drink, why would you try a single drink and give your enemy power again? … once you see the truth about drinking, the fear of never being able to drink again is replaced by the excitement of never having to drink again. The experience is euphoric. You see your entire life, long and healthy, stretch out before you. You are proud. You have done something amazing. You are excited to enjoy this remarkable life and all of the many, wonderful human experiences it holds." (Annie Grace, This Naked Mind)[10]

You are now Committed. And you understand the importance of dedicating time each day to work on yourself. As I mentioned in the previous chapter, you will use this time to get started on your SoberPractice. Your SoberPractice is the work, or habits, you will perform every day to achieve lasting sobriety and self-actualization. It makes sobriety the only worthwhile choice

---

10 Grace, Annie. *This Naked Mind: Control Alcohol, Find Freedom, Discover Happiness & Change Your Life.* Penguin Group, 2015.

in life. The second part of the SoberPractice, and the area you will focus on during the first month, is to Learn.

This is Your Brain on Bullshit

I don't know about you, but the thought of never drinking again used to terrify me. Not only did it seem extremely boring, but I hated the idea of being labeled an alcoholic for the rest of my life. Honestly, I saw no way out. I knew drinking wasn't working for me anymore. But I sure as hell didn't want to quit yet. How was I supposed to have a social life without alcohol? Oh, and everything I heard or saw about "recovery" looked downright depressing. It painted people like me as flawed and needing to spend the rest of our lives making amends. And to top it off, it seemed like recovering alcoholics were no longer allowed at the cool kids' table with the normies. No, we had given up our chance to enjoy one of life's greatest pleasures. In short, I used to view drinking alcohol as a positive thing. I thought it actually provided me with benefits, and I was scared to miss out on that.

Today, I know that those beliefs came from the massive amount of brainwashing I had been exposed to: the lies that tell us that drinking alcohol is actually a good thing, and that being sober is not an enjoyable way to live. I don't think I need to tell you that people in our society are exposed to this type of crap from a very young age. From the ads we see on TV, to the parents giving you that first sip, we are told that alcohol is a necessary part of the adult experience. We're told that it's fun, that it relieves stress, and that "everybody does it."

Take something as universal as the day you turn the arbitrary age of 21. While most people have already begun drinking at this age, it's still a rite of passage to get blasted on your 21st birthday.

In my family, drinking before that random day was looked down upon. But drinking on that day, and thereafter, was totally cool. Doesn't really hold up, right? They call it an "initiation into adulthood." Aren't we supposed to remember meaningful initiations and ceremonies? Aren't they supposed to mean something? I must have missed all that amidst the shots and vomit. It's pretty scary, really. And then we just laugh it off as the typical thing to do as young adults. It seems innocuous at the time, but this line of thinking stays with us well past our 21st birthday. We're taught to say no to drugs, but that drinking alcohol is cool. How screwed up is that?

Myths in a Bottle

We're also brainwashed to believe that we give up a genuine pleasure when we stop drinking, and that our life will somehow be less enjoyable without a drug. Replace the word "alcohol" with "heroin" in all of these types of statements, and it quickly becomes obvious how ridiculous they are. Would you ever assume someone's life is better because they shoot up every day? Or that it must be rough not being addicted to heroin anymore? Why does alcohol get the free pass? All in all, before we are adults, we are hammered with the message that drinking is the normal way to live, sobriety is somehow inferior, and that alcohol is the one drug that's okay.

To summarize, here are some of the myths we're made to believe about drinking:

- MYTH #1: Alcohol is good and a necessary part of society. It's what the grown-ups drink, and it is required to have a good time and relieve stress.

- MYTH #2: If you are under the age of 21, you shouldn't be drinking. If you are between the ages of 21 and 25, you are free to drink as much as you want. It's just college. If you are over the age of 25 and you drink too much, you have moral shortcomings. It's your fault that your drinking got this way. Shame on you!

- MYTH #3: Quitting drinking will not be easy, and you will no longer have the same quality of life drinkers have. You are an alcoholic, and in recovery, for life. The best you can hope for is the life of a typical AA member.

How would your life change if you no longer accepted these myths as true? What if you saw these lies as mere brainwashing, pushed by people who are hooked on alcohol and by the companies who profit from selling it to us? What if you discovered different and more accurate ways of thinking? What if you no longer believed that you need alcohol to have a good time? What if you accepted that drinking really isn't the elixir of life, or solver of problems, that it's made out to be? What if you found out that you didn't need to be a Bible toting AA member to achieve sobriety? Most importantly, what if you believed in your heart that getting sober could be the most meaningful commitment you've ever made, and that it could lead to a quality of life you didn't even know was possible? Adopting these beliefs is the goal of month one. It's what you need to Learn.

My Mental Turning Point

Early in my journey of getting sober, I stumbled across a book that got me thinking in a new way. It reversed the brainwashing I had forever been exposed to, and replaced it with the true facts of drinking. It all seems so obvious now, but when you are caught in the trap of alcohol addiction, seeing the substance and situation for what they are is earth shattering. I was so used to using alcohol as a crutch to get through the events of my life that I simply couldn't imagine another way of living.

In truth, alcohol is one of the most addictive substances in the world. It is a drug. It is also one of the most widely used drugs claiming more lives than all the other hard drugs combined. In truth, alcohol doesn't solve your problems. It merely provides a distraction to them as you wake up the next day hungover with the same issues. In truth, alcohol doesn't enable you to have a good time, and it surely doesn't make you more sociable or attractive.

Drinking makes you mentally, physically, emotionally, spiritually, and financially weaker. Seriously, how many times have you woken up from a night of drinking and really been glad you did it? Alcohol wastes your time and money, and it ruins your relationships. Most importantly, drinking alcohol is a habitual way to avoid problems in your life. Do it enough, and you will become addicted like I did. You will no longer have the ability to solve your problems. And you will be hooked on distracting yourself as additional problems mount.

The book I so luckily stumbled across is *Kick the Drink . . . Easily!* by Jason Vale. I will not go into the specific details here in order to not spoil the book, but Vale will change your mind in regards to drinking and sobriety. He will not only dull the effects of the brainwashing you've been exposed to. He will debunk the myths entirely. Vale speaks the truth about what drinking and alcohol addiction really are. The information may seem obvious to your high level conscious mind, but the intention of the book is to affect your subconscious mind, so that you significantly decrease, or lose altogether, your desire for drinking. And he will show you how great it is to be sober.

Conscious vs Subconscious Thinking

The thinking behind *Kick the Drink* is that we all know drinking is bad for us and that we should probably stop. Isn't that why you picked up this book? This is high level conscious thinking, and it takes place in the prefrontal cortex area of the brain. I say that it's conscious thinking because you are aware that you're thinking it. You could also think of this part of your brain as your conscience. The thoughts coming out of your prefrontal cortex are organized and deliberate. This part of your brain is also where planning, complex cognitive behavior, and decision making take place. It's the area you think of when you imagine the brain. It's relatively large in humans and responsible for much of our personality and decisions.

So we do our research on alcohol and decide it's not for us. We see the negative effects it's having on our lives and the population as a whole. We swear we will cut back or maybe even give up drinking entirely. We make all types of promises to ourselves. All of this makes sense because it falls in line with the high level information we have gathered in our prefrontal cortex.

But when Friday night rolls around, we still drink, right? So is our prefrontal cortex asleep on the job, or what? Is something wrong with us? Not at all. In fact, we do all kinds of things that we don't plan to do, things that don't make sense given our long-term goals, and things that don't fall in line with what's going on in our prefrontal cortex. So we continue drinking and suffering the terrible effects of alcohol. This confuses us and leaves us discouraged, hungover, and fed up at the end of our weekend bender. Why do we go against all that we know and desire? Why can't we walk the talk?

I'll tell you why. It's because there is another part of the brain that also plays a role in decision making. Relative to human evolution, it's an older part of the brain, often referred to as the "reptilian brain." Have you ever seen those cartoons where the main character has an angel on one shoulder and a devil on the other? Think of the angel as your prefrontal cortex and the devil as your reptilian brain. Your devil brain is the nucleus accumbens. It's the pleasure and reward center of your brain. It activates our motivation and allows willpower to translate into action. The nucleus accumbens is heavily triggered by dopamine, something alcohol and drugs supply in large doses.

But here's the kicker. Our reptile brain is predominantly subconscious and automatic. We don't even realize the triggers and motivations that are happening inside of us and springing us to action. And these forces are much stronger than anything that happens in our prefrontal cortex. That's why we still drink when we know that we shouldn't. Because the older, and more primitive, area of our brain overrides the newer and more complex area. Our animal instinct overcomes our conscience, and we become victims to our subconscious whims. This falls in line with the confusion you have probably experienced when you drink too much for the 34th time that year, and it helps explain the regret and despair you feel afterwards.

So it's not our fault, right? There's nothing we can do? Well, not exactly. What most people don't realize is that you can actually reprogram your subconscious mind. You can teach the devil on your left shoulder to obey the angel on your right shoulder. You do this by using your rational mind (prefrontal cortex) to alter the deeply embedded motivations within your reptile brain (nucleus accumbens). And this leads right back to the second part of the SoberPractice. This is the kind of Learning I'm talking about. *Kick the Drink* was written to help you adapt your subconscious mind, so that it starts working for you. This way you will want to stop drinking with every part of your brain.

We need to do more than listen to counselors and family members insisting we shouldn't drink. We know we shouldn't drink. We know all the damage it has done to our lives and how much better everything would be without it. But that reptile brain of ours still wants to drink. The devil wins out. That's because all the previously mentioned brainwashing has affected our subconscious mind. That, and the repeated bouts of heavy drinking that has flooded our system with on-demand dopamine hits over the years. We have become addicted to the pleasure and, in most cases, have built a tolerance to it.

But here is the good news. *Kick the Drink* doesn't just spit out the same tired facts regarding alcohol. You know all that. The book cuts through to the core of your problem: your deepest motivations. It speaks to the subconscious and automatic parts of your brain so you truly will not desire to drink. Finally, your strongest desires will align with your best intentions. You can finally commit to sobriety. And the best part is, it takes relatively little willpower to make this change.

HABIT: Read *Kick the Drink . . . Easily* for 20 minutes

So where are we at? You've committed to sobriety, and you are starting out on the first month of your SoberPractice. Now, you are about to begin loading the first habit that will change your life. That habit is to read *Kick the Drink* by Jason Vale. I would aim to read for about 20 minutes per day throughout the first month. This will debunk the false brainwashing once and for all, so that every part of your mind will be truly motivated to achieve sobriety. This should be the first thing you work on during your one hour of dedicated SoberPractice work. It really needs to be the priority. That way, you'll have the right attitude for the rest of the day ahead. If you believe that drinking is a positive thing, and that you are giving something up by quitting, you'll have a hard time getting sober. Even if you manage to withstand your cravings through sheer force of will, you will always feel deprived and lonely while watching other people drink. Either that, or you will eventually give in as the pressure mounts. This is the lose-lose predicament of recovery through AA. Not so with the SoberPower Method. To make a permanent change takes more than just conscious willpower. It takes a transforming of your subconscious beliefs. This is why reading *Kick the Drink* can help you get sober for the long term, so that you love your decision every day.

Once your brainwashing is reversed, you will know the truth and no longer desire to drink. Instead, you will desire to be sober and have the beautiful life that comes with it. With this mind-set (both conscious and subconscious), quitting drinking will become one of the most enjoyable experiences of your life. In fact, you will feel blessed that you no longer have to put a poison in your body just to get through the day. You'll be thrilled that you aren't a normy and don't have the baggage that comes with that lifestyle. You will wake up every day feeling amazing, and you'll feel pity for those who still believe in the "benefits" of an addictive toxin.

Now that I've read the book and have reversed my own brainwashing, I couldn't be happier to be a non-drinker. Just like the quote at the beginning of this chapter, I'm legitimately relieved to be done drinking. I'm excited for what life has in store for me, and I don't feel like a stigmatized alcoholic. In fact, I don't consider myself to be an alcoholic at all. I don't have time for those labels and stigmas. I've truly moved on. Instead, I feel like the luckiest person in the world who received one of life's ultimate cheat codes. Ever since I quit drinking, I really do feel like I'm living with SoberPowers.

For me, reading Jason Vale's book was the first step towards feeling this way. There is nothing that I could summarize on these pages that would come close to affecting your subconscious mind the way his book will. So please read *Kick the Drink* during the first month of your SoberPractice, and you'll be well on your way to Learning the truth as well. Just know that in the beginning, the battle between the angel on your left shoulder and the devil on the right will likely get a little messy. Your old beliefs will fight for their right to persist and survive. You simply have to be more persistent than they are, knowing that when this battle is over, *both* parts of your mind will be acting in your best interest.

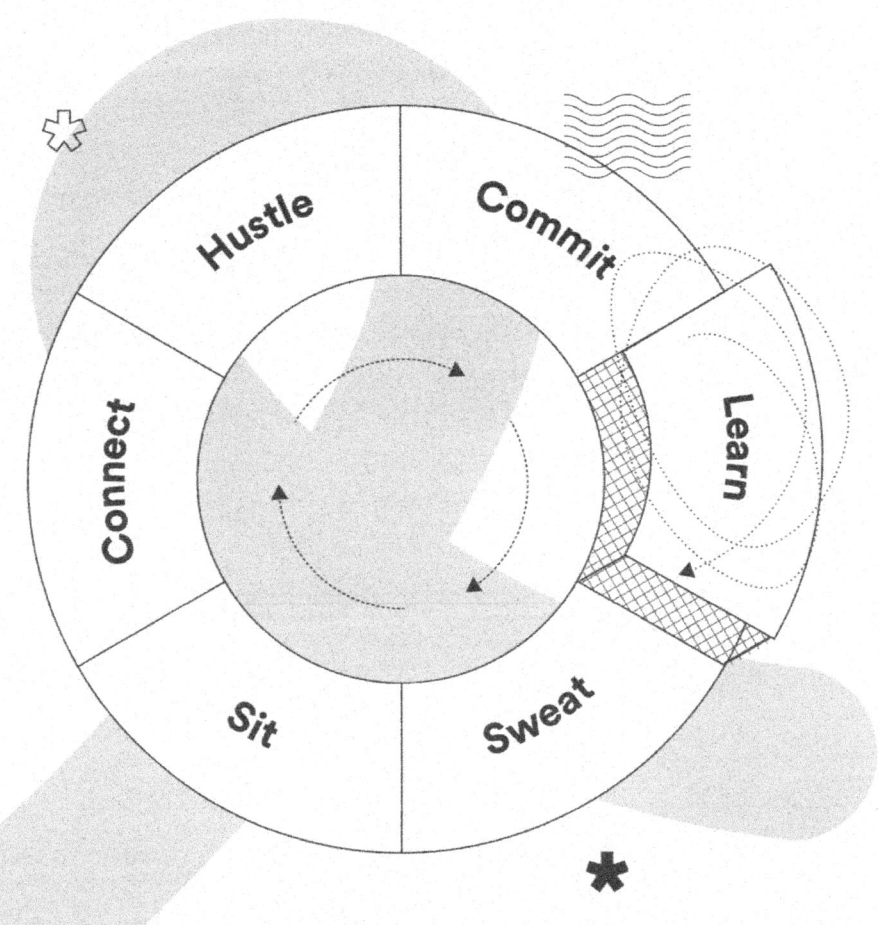

Month 1:
Learn
Read *Kick the Drink...Easily*
for 20 minutes

CHAPTER 7

SWEAT

"The key to lifelong happiness is to be a lifelong athlete." (John Dupuy, Integral Recovery)

At this point, you have learned the truth about alcohol and are seeing the many benefits of sobriety. And you'll be ready for the next area of your SoberPractice. After focusing on the habit of Learning during month one, you'll work on building up your body during the second month. It's time to Sweat. This doesn't mean that you forget, or stop working on, the habit you loaded during the first month. In fact, reading should be ingrained and part of your life at this point. You are in the maintenance phase with it, which requires significantly less discipline and willpower than the loading phase. Quite simply, the habit is now yours. So now, you can continue it with little effort, and use your willpower to load the Sweat habit. Ah, the beauty of habit building.

Put simply, the goal of month two is to feel physically amazing. Our bodies are beautiful machines. They're designed to thrive on this planet. So, the secret to good health is to get your body doing what it's meant to do. No extreme diets or workout gimmicks required. Read on, and you'll have more energy than ever before. To be honest, this is a good goal for sobriety in and of itself. Some people even stop at this point. But for people like us, who strive to be the best version of ourselves, it's about more than that. Having good physical health is one of the keys to unlocking our true potential.

Fat, Drunk, and Stupid

Throughout most of my twenties, my health was decent at best. I was your typical weekend warrior: eating healthy and training throughout the week only to throw away all progress during my weekend drinking excursions. What a waste, right? To spend 75 percent of my days in the gym and making sound dietary decisions, only to still be fat and overweight in the end. This is how I spent ten years of my life. Chubby and slightly out of shape.

While this was hardly a healthy or productive way to spend a decade, things only got worse. Much worse. When I turned 30, my drinking picked up. And not surprisingly, that's when I noticed my health begin to decline. As any problem drinker knows, the hangovers only get worse. Soon, they were accompanied by pain on my sides, high blood pressure, acid reflux, headaches, buzzing in my ears, dry skin, and more. I honestly don't remember all the different ailments I was dealing with. But there were many, and they seemed to keep popping up. When I couldn't keep my promises to slow down my drinking, things started to get scary. How much further would I take this? What would be the next issue? Would I be able to recover from it?

And then there was the horrible sleep. As any seasoned drinker knows, it's hard to stay on a consistent sleep schedule when you're constantly under the influence. You know how it is. You stay up late drinking. You wake up anxious. You don't have the discipline to follow any type of routine. Even worse, alcohol makes it so you don't get good rest even while you are sleeping. I remember waking up after ten hours of lying in bed, feeling like I hadn't slept for a single minute. Truly, I was physically exhausted as a drinker. I imagine that you feel the same way.

At the end of the day, none of this should have been a surprise to me. It certainly isn't now. Alcohol is a toxin. The second you drink it, your body tries to get rid of it as quickly as possible. By drinking alcohol regularly, you are poisoning yourself regularly. Looking at it from my current perspective, it's obvious that you cannot be physically fit as a regular drinker. The commercials showing healthy people drinking light beers on the beach are just more brainwashing and nonsense. Alcohol makes you fat, tired, and unhealthy. Period.

Flipping the Script

Thank god the nightmare is over for me. And soon, it will be for you as well. But I won't sugarcoat this. Getting healthy takes time. That's because, once again, it's all about building habits that work for you. When I got sober, I didn't go from sick to healthy overnight. It took a few weeks to start sleeping well again, but it happened. And it all started when I quit poisoning myself and started my SoberPractice. I got back into the gym and started making healthier eating decisions. My exercise and diet regimens were not strict by any means. But they were part of my SoberPractice, so they were consistent. And that's all that counts in this game.

Today, just two years after getting sober, I'm looking and feeling better than ever before. I have followed my SoberPractice the whole time. This means I have been exercising almost every day, eating as healthy as I can, and sleeping regularly for close to eight hours a night. All of this has undoubtedly been one of the driving forces behind me staying sober. But as I keep saying, it's a circular process. Getting sober makes it possible to be physically healthy, which in turn makes it much more enjoyable to be sober. It's yet another positive shift that occurs with the SoberPower Method. Getting fit is fundamental to that lifestyle change. But you gotta be willing to Sweat.

Nothing Feels Better Than Living in a Healthy Body

Honestly, it's been a lot of fun seeing this all happen. All of my major aches, pains, and hangover-related maladies were gone within days of getting sober—really everything. Imagine that for a moment. During the first six months, I lost 25 pounds. I'd been trying to lose that weight for years. It happened painlessly with the SoberPower Method. A lot of the credit goes to simply cutting out all the empty calories I'd been consuming through alcohol. The fat just melted away like magic. But as is always the case, my SoberPractice habits took it a step further.

I can't emphasize enough how good it feels to finally look fit. If you're having a hard time imagining this difference, try picking up a 25-pound weight and walking around your house with it for a few hours. You'll feel the difference. You might even feel it the next day. That's what it's like to be 25 pounds overweight. So if you've been struggling with low energy, or if you can't lose weight as a drinker, wait until you stop drinking. It's much easier. I'd been working out for over ten years to achieve a look I could only manage through cutting out alcohol.

Looks aside, my energy level has improved dramatically since I got sober. I have *positive* energy now. In the old days, it took me until Wednesday to finally feel like I'd sweated out all the booze from the previous weekend. I couldn't train or sleep under those conditions. Now my life is one constant stream of health and wellness. That's because my SoberPractice goes down seven days a week. Just imagine that. Instead of feeling groggy and hungover on Monday, you could feel rested and ready to attack another week. Imagine life with no three-day recovery periods. Imagine if every second you spent working out was actually pushing you forward, instead of making you feel horrible. And how would you like to look young again?

Getting Sober is Better Than Plastic Surgery

Even now, two years sober, I still get comments all the time about how healthy and young I look. That's because along with the weight loss and energy increase, my skin has cleared up. It pains me to write this, but I've even been told it's "glowing." My only regret is that I didn't get sober sooner! I hope I don't sound too superficial here. In reality, all of this is positive feedback about my new SoberPower lifestyle. That lifestyle can be yours. Getting fit is one of the most outward signs of being healthy and sober. The compliments you get from others will be a constant reminder of the positive trajectory your life is on.

Why spend so much time on the health benefits of sobriety? Because if you really want to quit drinking for good, you need to *see* some of the benefits of getting sober. One of the most surefire ways to do this is by improving your physical health. And you don't have to be the next Arnold Schwarzenegger to make this happen. You just have to follow your SoberPractice every day.

Anyone who has experienced hangovers and physical illness due to drinking will feel relieved and motivated once they turn this area of their life around. It will happen for you, too. Once you commit to sobriety, you'll be more than halfway there. And once you adopt the simple and healthy habits of exercise, diet, and sleep, you will see some of the same benefits I did.

Outside of looking healthy, the reduced stress and increased confidence that come with a high-performing body is difficult to overstate. Almost all of my relationships have improved, as people sense a certain level of health and energy in me that was not there before. All in all, it just feels good to know that I'm maximizing my health and the natural functioning of my own body. As I've said, having good physical health is one of the most outward ways to prove to yourself, and others, that you are on top of your game. I don't think I need to explain the science behind how exercise and eating right will change your life. The information is well documented, and you probably have heard enough of it already. Now you just need to take action and build habits. That's how SoberPowers work.

HABIT: Exercise for 30 minutes

In order to have a healthy body, you have to *move* your body. By movement, I mean something slightly more challenging than what you do in your everyday life. When it comes to working out, everyone is different. In the end, it doesn't really matter what you do. What matters is that it works for you, and that you are consistent. At a bare minimum, spend at least 30 minutes per day walking outside. This will get your heart rate up and have you burning calories. You could even buy a Fitbit or an Apple Watch to start tracking your steps and calories. 10,000 steps per day is a great goal in the beginning. If that's too much at first, start with 1,000 steps and build up from there.

If you are a bit more hardcore, or if you already have a workout routine you're involved with, get in the gym and get after it. Again, start small. Personally, I've been doing CrossFit for the past ten years. I like it because it's competitive and provides a full body workout. If you are interested in CrossFit or any other established workout program, stop by a class or find people who are already doing it. Maybe you'd like to learn ballroom dancing or boxing? Or you can join a jogging club. Find something you enjoy, and find people to do it with. There is nothing better than combining regular exercise with healthy social interactions.

Another option is to pick up a new sport. Since getting sober, I've learned to mountain bike, and I do it whenever I can. If absolutely none of this appeals to you, run and do body weight exercises a few times per week. If you can only do one push-up, that's a good place to start. Even if you can only do knee push-ups, just do them on a consistent basis. It's amazing how fit you can get from just pull-ups, push-ups, and bodyweight squats.

The main thing to remember is to actually do *something*. It doesn't really matter what it is. Just keep moving, every day, for at least 30 minutes. Start small, and build up when you are ready. That's how you will become healthy for the long haul.

A Note on Diet and Sleep

There are two other aspects of physical health that I want to mention. In all honestly, they are just as important as exercise, but it is more difficult to think of them as concrete habits. They are more ongoing lifestyle changes that you should make to improve your health. The two aspects are diet and sleep. Both are super important, and I'd recommend examining each as you embark on your sober journey. But I didn't include them here as neither are something you would fit into an hour of SoberPractice work. That work makes up the core of the SoberPower Method, so that's what I want to emphasize in this book.

The other reason I didn't include diet and sleep as habits is because I think that by cutting out alcohol, these things tend to take care of themselves. If you aren't getting hammered all the time, chances are you're going to eat a bit healthier. If you aren't hungover and anxious, I bet you're going to be sleeping better. So I left them off the habit list. But feel free to add them onto *your* SoberPractice if you'd like. If you're interested, here's a head start.

Real Food

Eating healthy seems daunting as hell these days, right? First off, there are more diets out there than I could possibly list in this book. Most of them are just sales gimmicks devised by the same type of people who think drinking is a good idea. So ignore all that and things become less intimidating.

The truth is, eating healthy is all about eating *real food*. By real food, I mean anything that is not processed. If you're unsure what this means, try reading the food labels and see how many of the ingredients you recognize as coming directly from a plant or an animal. For example, vegetables, meat, fruit, nuts, and rice have very simple ingredient lists. But stay away from chips and soda as often as possible. There's a reason you don't find those items growing on trees. The same goes for any food where the ingredients sound like they could be on your shampoo bottle. One piece of helpful advice I always try to follow is to shop around the perimeter of the grocery store. That's where the real food is. The aisles are where healthy eating decisions go to die.

But yeah, throw some cheat days in there. I sure do, and if you've read this far, you deserve it. But make real food your primary source of calories. If you are struggling with this, I suggest using the same strategy we did with exercise above. Start small. Try just eating a healthy breakfast at first. Then cut out unhealthy snacking. Once this becomes normal, you can do the same thing for the rest of your meals. As your energy level increases and you begin to look more fit, you will probably find that you actually enjoy eating healthy. That's the start of a very healthy lifestyle. Combine this with consistent exercise, and your body will start healing itself. Just like mine did.

Catching Z's

One of the most important things you can do for yourself is to make high quality sleep a priority. Aim for at least seven hours per night, but the goal should be eight for most of us. To find your ideal amount, see how long you sleep before waking up without an alarm clock. Try this for a few days, and make sure you are waking up rested and energized. Record everything. Boom! Now you know your sleep requirements.

The best way to get your ideal amount of sleep is to follow a strict sleep schedule. What this really means is going to bed at the same time every day. Most people understand the idea of getting up at a set hour. We don't have a choice with our jobs and responsibilities. But few people establish a regular bedtime. They stay up too late watching TV and drinking wine, leaving themselves exhausted the next day. So figure out what time you need to be up to start your SoberPractice, and go to bed around eight hours earlier (or whatever your sleep requirement is). That's how to be rested. And it's also how to build a successful SoberPractice. It all works together in building your SoberPowers.

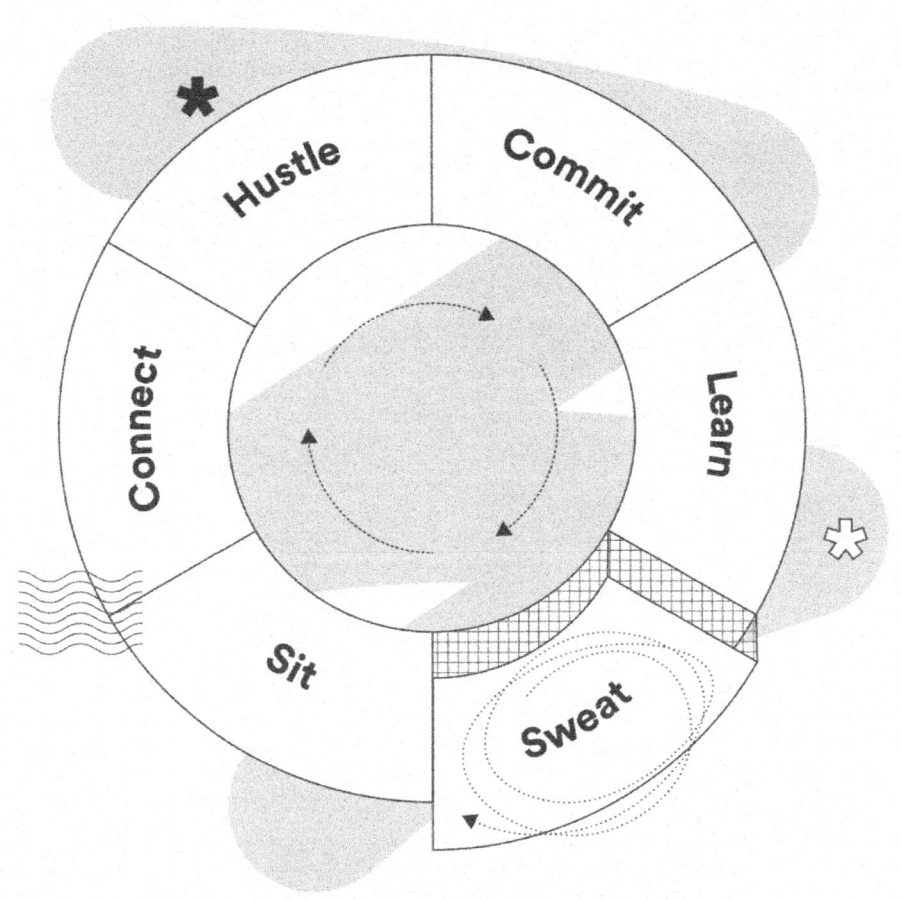

Month 2:
Sweat
Exercise for 30 minutes

CHAPTER 8

SIT

"Why does no one admit his failings? Because he's still deep in them. It's the person who's awakened who recounts his dream, and acknowledging one's failings is a sign of health." (Seneca, Letters from a Stoic)

You are now entering the third month of your SoberPractice. You have successfully loaded the habits of reading (learning the truth) and exercising. The focus during month three is to learn to feel gratitude and acceptance in your everyday life. For the next few pages, I will refer to the combination of these two feelings as "spirituality". I realize the word spirituality is loaded, and that it means different things to different people. Feel free to discard the word and replace it with whatever suits you.

Spirituality? Are You Serious?

Regardless of your religious background, your goal should be to feel a combination of gratitude and acceptance every day. This will take practice, and at first it will feel like you're never going to get it. But think of it like riding a bike. The first time you try, it feels like you're totally out of control and off balance. However, with enough training and discipline, it becomes second nature. Pretty soon, it's hard to imagine that there was ever a time that you *couldn't* ride a bike. Know what I mean? Well, it's the same thing when training your mind to feel gratitude and acceptance.

These two emotions build off your work from month one (learning the truth from *Kick the Drink)*. In a crazy way, learning to feel gratitude is a whole lot like seeing through brainwashing and lies. The same systems are at play. It's one thing to say you are gracious and accepting of your life. It's another thing to *truly feel it* in the present moment. Once again, you have to bypass your conscious thinking. You probably know that you have a lot to be thankful for, and you also probably know that it would be a good thing to feel thankful. But in order to actually experience gratitude, you have to convince your subconscious brain. The best method I know for doing this is a meditation practice. The key word is *practice*. Fake it until you make it. Actively think about things you are thankful for, until one day, you wake up feeling gratitude for everything.

Confession: My Unfaithful Past Relationship with Meditation

For most of my life, I've been drawn to meditation. Since the word "meditation" has been butchered extensively by mainstream society, let me provide a super brief description. Meditation was originally a Buddhist practice. There are many ways to meditate, but the primary goal of meditation is to quiet the mind and focus on the present moment only. That means not thinking about the past or the future. It means accepting your life as it is *right now*. Common ways to practice this are through focusing on your breath or "watching" thoughts come and go. It all leads to the same thing. Acceptance of the present moment.

I started reading books on meditation during college and attempted to practice regularly throughout my twenties. I didn't get very far. Being a heavy drinker made this very difficult. Back when I was drinking, my meditation practice was inconsistent at best. There was no way I was going to sit on a cushion while under the influence or hungover. So my meditation practice sat on the back burner. I only practiced on rare occasions, when I had the willpower to quiet my mind. Honestly, it was probably only a few times per month.

Needless to say, in spite of my dabbling in meditation, my spiritual life sucked. As usual for me back then, alcohol was getting in the way. When you are in active addiction, your only concern is yourself. Most of my time was spent either drinking, trying to get over a hangover, or trying to catch up with life during the brief moments in between. And then there was the constant shame and regret. There is just no way to entertain any type of spiritual life when you feel that crappy all the time. Outside of all the physical ailments I described in the previous chapters, my state of mind was largely a negative one filled with dread and embarrassment. I wasn't proud of the way I was living, and I wasn't excited for where I was headed. I felt little to no gratitude for being alive, and I wasn't accepting of most aspects of my life.

On a more fundamental level, when you are addicted to something, you are chasing the pleasurable dopamine rush it provides. It doesn't matter if it's alcohol, sex, or your iPhone, the motivations and processes of addiction are all the same. From the perspective of a meditator, you are caught in the trance of chasing pleasure and avoiding pain. This is a very bad place to be, and as a matter of experience, it is the very opposite of acceptance. The dopamine high creates a corresponding low that compels you to "fix" the feeling with a substance or an experience. This is how the cycle of addiction reinforces itself. This was the life I was living two years ago, and it was not a spiritual one. I repeat—you simply cannot live a spiritual life if you are addicted. This is because you are forever chasing something that will not last. And you are not accepting of the present moment. Drinking cannot quench a spiritual thirst for the same reason junk food cannot satisfy real hunger. Eventually, you'll come down from that bender, and your nightmare will continue.

During my early days of getting sober, things didn't get much better. Not right away at least. I felt like a total failure and was embarrassed to admit that I had a problem with alcohol. Although I wasn't drinking Tiger Blood on YouTube, my downfall was fairly visible to my family, friends, and co-workers. It still makes me cringe to this day. Truly, the first few weeks were my darkest. I didn't know what SoberPowers were. I was afraid my feelings of dread and anxiety would be the new normal now that I was done drinking. Maybe you can relate. Lucky for me, there were ways to move beyond the negative thinking. And it all started with getting back into meditation. A new life outlook was right around the corner, and it started with training my mind to feel gratitude and acceptance.

Finding Your Own Way Forward

Once I removed alcohol from my life *and* began my SoberPractice, I had the time and energy to get my spiritual life back on track. As I said, the early days of sobriety may be uncomfortable for you.

They sure as hell were for me. But there were also moments of incredible joy and gratitude mixed in with the fear. At the very least, I wasn't hungover anymore. And because I was seeing past the brainwashing and lies, I knew that a hangover was something I'd never experience again. And that is truly something to feel grateful for.

In my early days of sobriety, waking up without a hangover was enough to spark feelings of awe and gratitude. I had totally forgotten how good it feels to simply be alive! For some of you, it might take some time to experience these feelings and get over the numbness brought on by your addiction. That's okay, as all good things take time. But you can also speed up the process through active work. When I decided to get SoberPowers, I loved how meditation didn't require someone constantly telling me what to do (see: AA). I had enough of that growing up. Meditation made my spiritual practice *mine*. It allowed me to discover *my own* way forward.

Pretty soon, I was meditating every day. I haven't stopped since. Building this consistency has been huge for my spiritual life. It has allowed me to feel both gratitude and acceptance. This is because focusing on the present moment during meditation makes you more mindful. You experience life as it is: *right here, right now*. And you realize there is nothing to do. You are amazing just the way you are. It takes some time, but meditation teaches you to enjoy the present moment instead of searching for another fix. And it teaches you to accept the problems in your life instead of avoiding them. Trust me, I know this sounds crazy. But give it some time. Through consistent practice, you may actually begin to believe it.

A consistent meditation practice, however, is only the start of my new and improved spiritual life. Overall, I just feel so much more grounded and purposeful than ever before. I'm living a more virtuous life based on my values instead of my self-centered pleasure centers. I'm finally off the roller coaster of using an addictive substance to chase pleasure and avoid pain. It's that simple, and knowing this creates so much confidence within me. I now make decisions to maximize the long-term well-being of myself and those around me. This is a far cry from the days of constantly causing and nursing hangovers. But it starts with training your mind to feel gratitude and acceptance. Again, this will take time and persistence.

It's also important to note that not every day is perfect for me. Even as a sober person, life still has its ups and downs. But I am accepting of the ups and downs now. Because that's life. And I really don't need anything more than that. So I'm not only accepting of the bad days that will inevitably come, but I'm grateful for them. Things could have ended up so much worse for me. I could still be drinking! I'm truly grateful to be alive and sober. You will be, too.

HABIT: Meditate for 15 minutes

You may be thinking, "Congratulations, you tree-hugging hipster, but I've never meditated before. With all of this sobriety stuff on my plate, how am I supposed to start now?"

I'm going to give you the same answer I did regarding exercise: start small. You can even start with one minute of meditation at first. Then build up from there. Since learning to feel gratitude and acceptance is a major part of the SoberPractice, I suggest working up to about 15 minutes per day. That's a solid habit right there.

If you are an experienced meditator, you probably won't need much help here. If you are new and interested, I would recommend getting one of the amazing meditation apps on your phone. Headspace, Calm, and Waking Up are just a few of my favorites. They will walk you through the entire experience. These apps also allow you to track your progress so you can be sure that meditation becomes a habit. If you don't want to spend a couple dollars per month on this, there are plenty of meditation videos for free on YouTube. If you don't want to use technology to meditate (completely understandable), just sit on a chair with your eyes closed, set a timer, and focus on your breath. If a thought or a worry enters your mind, simply acknowledge it (without reacting to it), and go back to your breathing. It's that simple.

Oh, and here's another thing. You don't even have to meditate to experience gratitude and acceptance. There are other ways to go about this:

- Journaling. Sitting and writing gives you time to explore the contents of your own mind so you can recognize what needs to change. More importantly, it will help you discover the things you need to be grateful for, and the things you need to accept. Another great way to get after this is to start a gratitude journal. Information for this type of journaling can be found online. The *Five Minute Journal* is another great option. If none of this appeals to you, simply write down five things per day that you are grateful for. They can be anything. This may seem silly at first, but pretty soon your mindset will shift, and you will begin to feel more gratitude.

- Prayer. If you are already active in a specific religion, rekindle your relationship with it. It seems to me that feeling gratitude is an underlying theme for most major religions. So if you favor a specific faith, or have a good background in one already, practice it in a way that suits you.

A Healthy Mind is a SoberPower

At this point, you'll have come a long way. Looking over the past three months, by reading *Kick the Drink,* you will get smarter and see things more clearly. Your subconscious mind will shift, and you will no longer desire to drink. Exercising will get you fit and full of positive energy. Through prayer, meditation, or journaling, you will experience gratitude and acceptance. You will be well on your way to being both a sober *and* happy person, as your formerly addicted mind becomes focused and clear. Instead of being at war with itself, your mind will be peaceful, accepting, and productive.

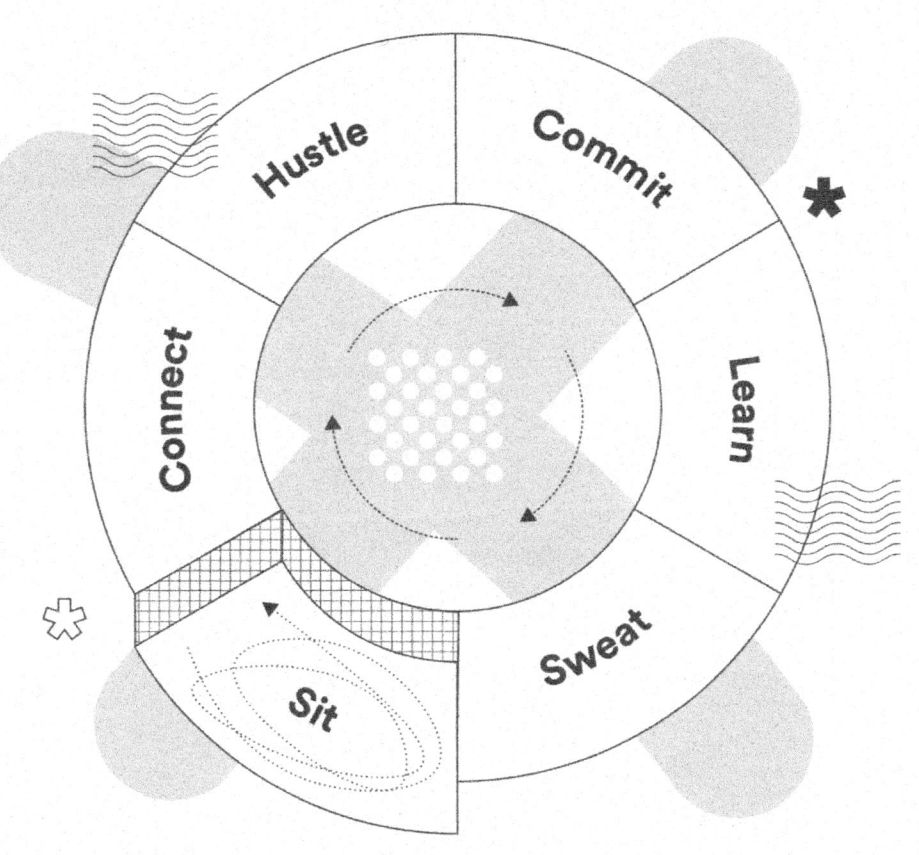

Month 3:
Sit
Meditate for 15 minutes

CHAPTER 9

CONNECT

=====================================

"Human beings, fundamentally, are distinctly, spectacularly social. Lonely and isolated, we cannot survive, let alone thrive." (Belong, Radha Agrawal)

At this point you'll have been working on your SoberPractice for three months. Just a guess, but I think you'll be feeling much better. Hell, maybe even a little confident. You'll have officially loaded the habits of reading, exercise, and meditation. Just think how many people are trying to master even *one* of those! Truly, those three habits are some of the greatest building blocks of success. But are we going to stop there? Nah. This is month four and the name of the section is Connect. What do I mean by that? So far, you've been going it alone. It's time to change all that. This month is all about finding like-minded people and connecting openly with them.

The Average of Five Drinking Buddies

You're about to be a newly sober person. I get it. If you are anything like I was, you've had some pretty shitty relationships over the years. Those people are probably still hanging around. You probably had a lot of drinking buddies, but very few true friends. You've probably also stepped on a few people while putting your drinking first. Some of these bad relationships might have even driven you to drink in the first place. And since that only made the situation worse, you drank even more, and the cycle repeated itself. Thankfully, you are now getting off this horrible roller coaster. You're going to be healthier and more present. You'll be ready to start repairing your relationships and, in some cases, replace them with better ones.

As they say, you are the average of the five people you spend the most time with. As drinkers, we hung out with people who acted the same way we did. Meaning that most of our friends were other problem drinkers who justified and encouraged our behavior. Trust me, this isn't the best strategy for long-term happiness and success. Truly, hanging around negative people will make you a negative person. And make no mistake, as a heavy drinker, you are having that same effect on others. During our drinking days, we brought other people down, and were in turn brought down by them. It was a vicious cycle of negativity, and the only way out is to get sober and change these relationships.

But it goes even deeper. When you think about it, just about any negative emotional state you can have is enhanced, or even caused, by your relationships with other people. Just think about all the times you've had anxiety. Wasn't it because you were worried about how others would view you? Wasn't it because you were concerned with how you would fit in, and how your life would turn out in comparison to others? How about the times you were depressed? Wasn't this at least partially due to the negative interactions you were having with others? I'm not saying the quality of your relationships is the only determining factor of your emotional health, but I think it is the primary one. That is why I believe that the majority of your emotional problems will vanish once you surround yourself with high quality people and begin the process of having open and authentic relationships with them.

Vulnerability is the Way Forward

The secret to having healthy relationships is a willingness to make yourself vulnerable. Once you find positive people you can be vulnerable around, your anxiety and depression (two triggers for drinking alcohol) will greatly diminish, and they will be replaced by a sense of emotional well-being. We have all felt that sense of peace and calm when we open up to someone who isn't out to judge or compete with us. Good people will allow you to do this. They will also reciprocate by trusting you with their internal lives. This might sound hard to believe if you don't have these kinds of people in your life. But like gratitude, it's something you'll be fully convinced of once you experience it for yourself. And like gratitude, it takes some practice to build the habit.

Some of you might be weirded out hearing me praise the benefits of being open and vulnerable. I know I used to drink specifically to avoid these types of interactions. You may have done the same. But let me clarify that when I say "vulnerability," I'm talking about being who you really are, instead of always trying to impress others. I'm talking about being honest, instead of always trying to hide your imperfections. We all have challenges in life, and everything is much easier if we aren't ashamed of it. Being open will give others the chance to help you, and it will allow you to return the favor.

But didn't Darwin say life is all about competition? I get it. Humans evolved with many of these tendencies. But look where it's left a huge percentage of people—addicted, anxious, and miserable. It's time to evolve and move on. Being real always makes you more vulnerable. And if you surround yourself with positive people, vulnerability will go from being terrifying to being liberating.

I'll also add that laying your feelings and problems out in the open is the definition of being charismatic. Although we tend to think of vulnerability as a weakness, and assume that it reveals the chinks in our armor, it usually has the opposite effect. By revealing your true self to others, you gain their trust and confidence. Again, it's all a matter of choosing good relationships instead of toxic ones. Mature people will respect you for being vulnerable since most people don't have the guts to even try. Just imagine being surrounded by positive people who respect and trust you *because* you're showing them who you really are. It doesn't get much better than that. And you can build an amazing social circle this way.

Liquid Courage vs Real Courage

I think you know where I'm going here. During my drinking days, my relationships and emotions were a total mess. At the time, I was going through a breakup, so my confidence was at an all-time low. Instead of opening up to people about the breakup, and other issues I was having, I turned to alcohol. Drinking was a great crutch for me in this way. Instead of processing my life (both good and bad) with others in a healthy way, I drank. I tried to manage my issues and feelings by myself, in a social vacuum. That is why I couldn't move on from the breakup or grow in any meaningful way while using alcohol. So drinking, something that was supposed to improve my social life, kept me emotionally stagnant and feeling like crap.

During my heaviest drinking days, going out for drinks was just about the only thing I did with other people. All my friends were drinking buddies, and the general vibe was a negative one. Even in the presence of others, I truly felt alone. I just didn't feel like I could relate to anybody, because I wasn't willing to open up. It's funny, that looking back, I used to think you couldn't have a social life without alcohol. Now that I'm sober, I realize that alcohol was the very thing keeping me from having a healthy social life. It kept me from hanging out with people who did more than just sit around a table and drink, and it shut down my natural ability to be open, helpful, and charismatic.

Because I was not connecting with others, I slid into a deep depression and my anxiety levels shot through the roof. I felt like everyone was constantly judging and criticizing me. And I couldn't recognize any type of support system. I also believed that I would never find another woman who would love me. Honestly, none of this was true at all. It just seemed like it since I was so emotionally isolated from those around me. I didn't see it then, but it's all so obvious now. The thing that was supposed to give me courage and confidence had turned me into a shell of my true self.

It Ain't Over!

One of the best parts of getting sober has been rekindling all my old relationships. Honestly, it feels like I'm a brand new new person starting fresh with my friends. Sure, I've met a bunch of people during the past two years, but getting back on firm ground with people I've known my whole life has been by far my favorite change. Instead of being a drag on my friends and family, I truly believe that I've been an inspiration to them. Everyone has rough spots in their life, and some people succumb to them. But I have shown others that reinventing yourself is possible. And I'm totally willing to talk and be vulnerable about it. Now, instead of looking at my past with regret and shame, I see it was an opportunity for growth. That is what I believe now, and that is what I share with others. Oh, and I'm more present and a better listener than ever before. I'm there for my people now instead of being a drag. I'm finally normal again.

I'd also like to remind you that being vulnerable is what got me sober to begin with. In my darkest moment, it was that phone call and admission to my boss that finally set me free. That vulnerable moment was my first step in sobriety. It set in motion a chain of events that has changed my entire life. It has also set the tone for how I handle problems and relate with others. I'm more open and direct than I used to be. I'm more confident. And my relationships with my boss and colleagues are better than ever before.

On top of reconnecting with old friends, I've made it a point to go out into the world and meet new people. But not just anybody. I'm looking for people who have a positive outlook on life, put their health and success first, and have a growth mindset. During the past two years, my circle of friends has increased, and I have found others who are similarly motivated like me. Now, instead of drinking buddies, I have music friends, workout partners, business associates, mentors, and mentees. The list goes on. It's been great to see that there really is a social life out there for us sober people. Indeed, it's a much better one. All this proves that the willingness to be vulnerable is a sign of strength and personal resolve. You'll see what I mean when you take this step for yourself.

Social Connections as an Emotional Wellspring

It is truly amazing what connecting with positive people does for you emotionally. Gone are the days of constant depression and anxiety. Removing a toxic substance from my body was definitely a big reason for this, but reconnecting with my friends and family is right up there. And it really hasn't been that hard. I just make it a point to connect with at least one person on a genuine and deep level every day. One phone call is all it takes. Show up on that phone call as your real and authentic self, and you'll see miraculous things happen.

While we're on the subject of vulnerability, let me give you a demonstration by admitting that this is still the hardest step for me in the SoberPower Method. Opening up to others has always been difficult for me. I've always been the type of person who tries to deal with problems on my own. I guess I don't want others to see my weaknesses. And even to this day, when I find myself being guarded and closed with other people, my social anxiety creeps back in. It's nowhere near what it was during my drinking days, but it still sucks, especially now that I know it's my own doing. But with this knowledge has also come the realization that I can fix the problem in an instant. The second I open back up, my social anxiety vanishes without a trace. It's truly remarkable how this works.

HABIT: Open up with someone for 10 minutes

During the fourth month of your SoberPractice, the habit you need to build is vulnerability. Aim to connect with a positive person in your life for ten minutes each day. You are a newly sober person with a new outlook on life, so there is plenty to talk about. Tell them about your experience. How are you feeling and what are your difficulties? What are your goals for the future? Tell them how much you care about them. If you are anything like me, you neglected your most important relationships while turning to alcohol as your only friend. You've probably got a few people in your life who would love to hear from you. So it's time to rejoin society. Once you get the hang of connecting with people who already know you, you can take things a step further and start meeting new people. Find your ideal community of people who will support you in life and on your SoberPower journey. This will take time and confidence. So start by fixing what's already around you, and take things slowly from there. There is no rush here.

What you could do is make a list of all the people you've been meaning to talk to over the past weeks, months, or years. Who have you fallen out of touch with? Who have you neglected during your drinking years? Who would you like to build a relationship with in the future? Make this list, and meet with these people during the next month. Or just give them a quick ten minute phone call to check in. When you do reach out, keep it open and authentic. You don't have to go into every last detail of your life, but push your boundaries a bit and see what happens. Most likely, you have been bottling things up for a while. So I guarantee it will feel great to let go. Spend ten minutes per day connecting with others, and you'll see what I mean.

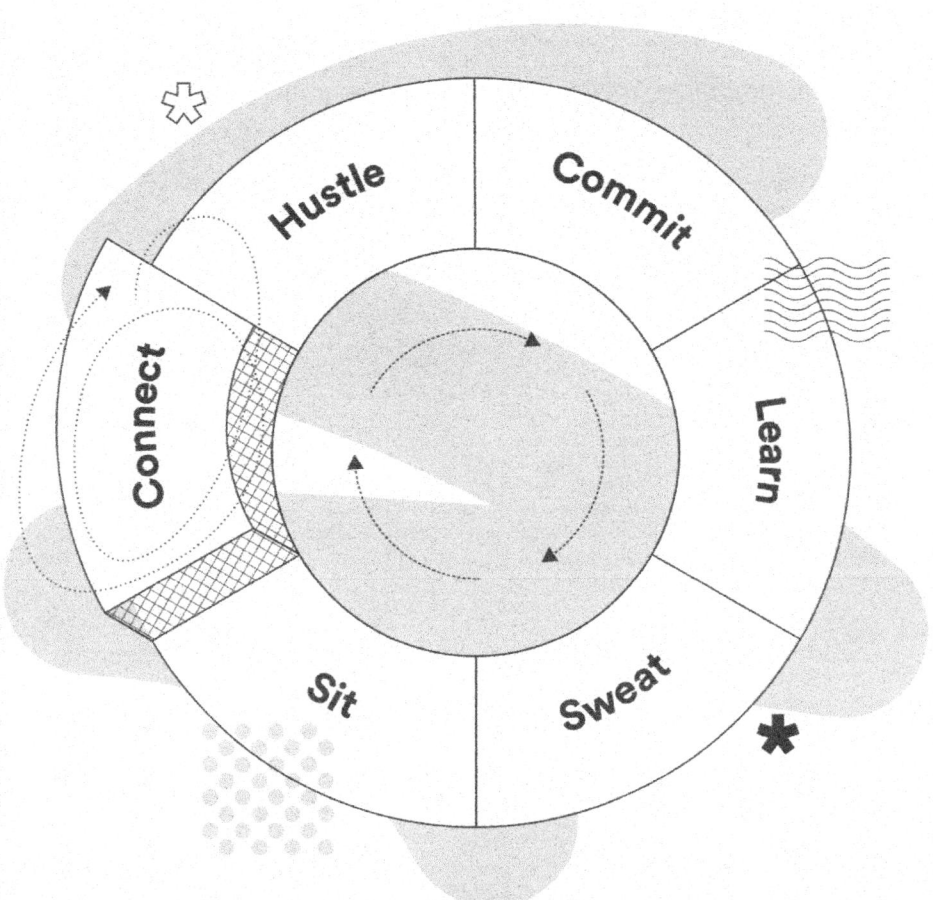

Month 4:
Connect
Open up with someone for 15 minutes

CHAPTER 10

HUSTLE

"It is crucial to rediscover a sense of purpose in life, to have a mission in the world, to be able to give one's unique gifts to the [cosmos]. Some higher meaning or value must become more important than the immediate gratification that comes from using drugs or alcohol, whether it is art, a meaningful career, or serving others." (John Dupuy, Integral Recovery)

Now we are on to the final part of the SoberPower Method. This is the fifth month of your SoberPractice, and at this point, you'll have built up some amazing habits to take with you on your journey. It is my hope that you will be sober *and* loving it. When you get to month five, you are seeing past the brainwashing and feeling grateful. You've also been building the habits to get physically healthy. I would guess that you are looking and feeling better than you have in years. And then, there are all the great people you are connecting with on a consistent basis. Truly, you'll be in a much better spot than you were four short months ago. That leaves us with the final part of the SoberPower Method and your daily SoberPractice: Hustle. That means figuring out what's meaningful to you, and pursuing it. This is the time to move beyond yourself. This is the time to build a life filled with purpose and intention, so that your sobriety and habits make the world a better place.

Becoming Your Own SoberHero

The purpose of the Hustle stage is to discover what your life mission is so that you can finally get after it. This seems like a lot, I know. So I will preface this section by saying that this part of your SoberPractice can come at a later time if you aren't ready for this type of work just yet. Your main goal right now is to gain your SoberPowers. Hopefully, by the fifth month you are well on your way to feeling that confidence. Once you have it, your life purpose will become clearer. That said, if you need to focus on continuing to get mentally, physically, and spiritually healthy, keep working there, and take it slow. As you know by now, the name of the game is finding long term success through consistent habits.

One of the biggest themes of living with SoberPowers is constant growth. By giving up alcohol, you are moving on from an ineffective version of yourself. By getting in the gym and eating right, you are growing physically. Through meditation and other spiritual practices, you will grow spiritually. By connecting with others, you'll grow emotionally. To truly thrive after you give up drinking, you have to develop the grow-or-die mentality. And when the time is right, you have to look beyond yourself. This will be the next step in your SoberPower evolution. You do it by making time each day to follow your passions. By finding out what your *it* is. And you will find *it* at the intersection of what you are good at, what you enjoy doing, and what you can do for other people.

When you find what your mission is, and start working towards it, you are going to feel great about being alive and sober. Your life will be about more than just making *you* better. It will be about making the *world* better. Because you are busy with your most important work, you will achieve levels of focus and concentration you previously thought impossible. You will quite simply be operating on a different mental plane than ever before, and you will realize that none of this would have been possible during your drinking days.

Survival Mode

It would be hard to look at my previous life as a time of growth. If I'm being honest, it felt like I was just trying to survive. My goal was simply to get through the day. As I've said, I was on the roller coaster of being either drunk or hungover. During the brief periods of time between bouts of drinking, I would frantically try to repair the damage I'd just created and get my life back on track. I was barely making the cut at work, so I hardly had the time to grow mentally or get after the things I loved in life. I just did enough to fund my drinking habit.

From a mental standpoint, I wasn't in a good place at all. My mind wasn't even close to performing at its best. We all know that you are not sharp when you are constantly drunk and hungover. Those days, I suffered from constant headaches and anxiety. I couldn't focus. Even simple tasks at work had to be put off until the hangover was gone. And that was just the easy day-to-day stuff. I couldn't even be bothered to think strategically.

On a more fundamental level, my mind was stuck. I wasn't spending any of my time learning new things or pursuing my passions. I barely even had passions back then. Sure, I had some vague goals, but I rarely thought about them, and I wasn't getting any closer to achieving them. This brought on feelings of shame from the moment I woke up in the morning. It felt like I was squandering my one life on this earth. And I was. Years went by when I made no progress in my life at all.

HABIT: Do Your Most Important Work for 30 minutes

Once I made the decision to get sober, it took time to get this part of my life on track. You may have the same experience. You probably have a lot going on right now, both internally and externally, and that's okay. Give your body and mind some time to adjust and heal. This is hardly being stuck. This is just getting yourself ready for what lies ahead. This is why you should take some time to relax and to get your mind and body right before you start thinking about your most important work. That's what I did. I read *Kick the Drink* and meditated everyday. I got in the gym and spent time with my family. Slowly but surely, my passions returned, and a vision for my life came into focus.

Doing your most important work means following your passions and the vision you have for your life. This is what you were put here to do. Once I had a clear direction for my life, I went to work with a focused mind. In the beginning, I spent about 30 minutes a day working on these passion projects as part of my morning SoberPractice. Then I got into a groove and increased that time to an hour. This may seem like a lot of work, but it won't feel like it to you. Spending some time each day to do your most important work, with a healthy and focused mind, is one of the most fulfilling habits you can develop.

Today, I've been pursuing my mission for close to two years. And I've made some genuine progress on work that is important to me. I've also developed skills that I had only dreamed of having as a drinker. The best part is, all of this stuff doesn't just make me better, it makes everyone *around* me better. One of the results of this daily work is the book you are reading right now. I have a few different projects I'm working on at the moment, but helping others achieve sobriety is one of the best. Sure, it's still a work in progress, and probably always will be. But it makes me jump out of bed in the morning thankful as hell that I'm sober, have a purpose, and am using my energy to help others. These days are so much different than my drinking days. I know that it will be the same for you.

The added bonus of pursuing your passions every day is that it changes your mindset. For example, I no longer feel dull and anxious on the regular. You won't either. I wake up feeling energetic and focused to take on whatever life throws at me. You will too. And since I'm doing my most important work in the morning, the day-to-day stuff comes easily. You'll discover this for yourself once you get started. Remember, when I was drinking, I could barely even get the easy stuff handled. Now, I am able to focus on my work and get things done. My memory has improved, and I learn new concepts much quicker. To be honest, I almost take it for granted how sharp I feel. It's a far cry from the old days of showing up to work (and life) hungover and unable to function. It will be the same for you. You'll see.

As I mentioned, this last part of your SoberPractice can come a bit later on as you load and internalize the previous four habits.

You'll know when the time has come to start doing your most important work. Once you are ready, the best way to get started is to dedicate 30 minutes of your SoberPractice to pursuing your passions. It's best to start with a small amount of time so you can turn this into a daily habit.

What you do during these 30 minutes is entirely up to you. Maybe you already have an important project that has been sitting on the back burner. If that's the case, start working on it. Move things forward every day. If you have no clue what you want to do, you can start by researching your areas of interest. This can be as simple as reading a book or listening to a podcast on a subject you're passionate about. Listen to your heart here, and take whatever step makes the most sense for you. Meditation can help here as well. Most importantly, do things you like to do and don't listen to anybody else. You didn't have time for this during your drinking days, but you do now. It is my experience that your purpose will become apparent to you as you continue to get your life back on track.

The Road to Clarity and Authentic Confidence

Once you start pursuing your passions and taking control of your life, I guarantee you will feel more mental clarity and confidence. Your anxiety levels will plummet once you know you are no longer squandering your days. Your focus will increase once you've developed the habit of doing your most important work every day. You will no longer be avoiding your calling in life. You will be present and actively engaged with it, and because of this

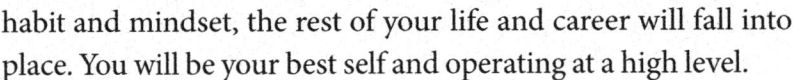

habit and mindset, the rest of your life and career will fall into place. You will be your best self and operating at a high level.

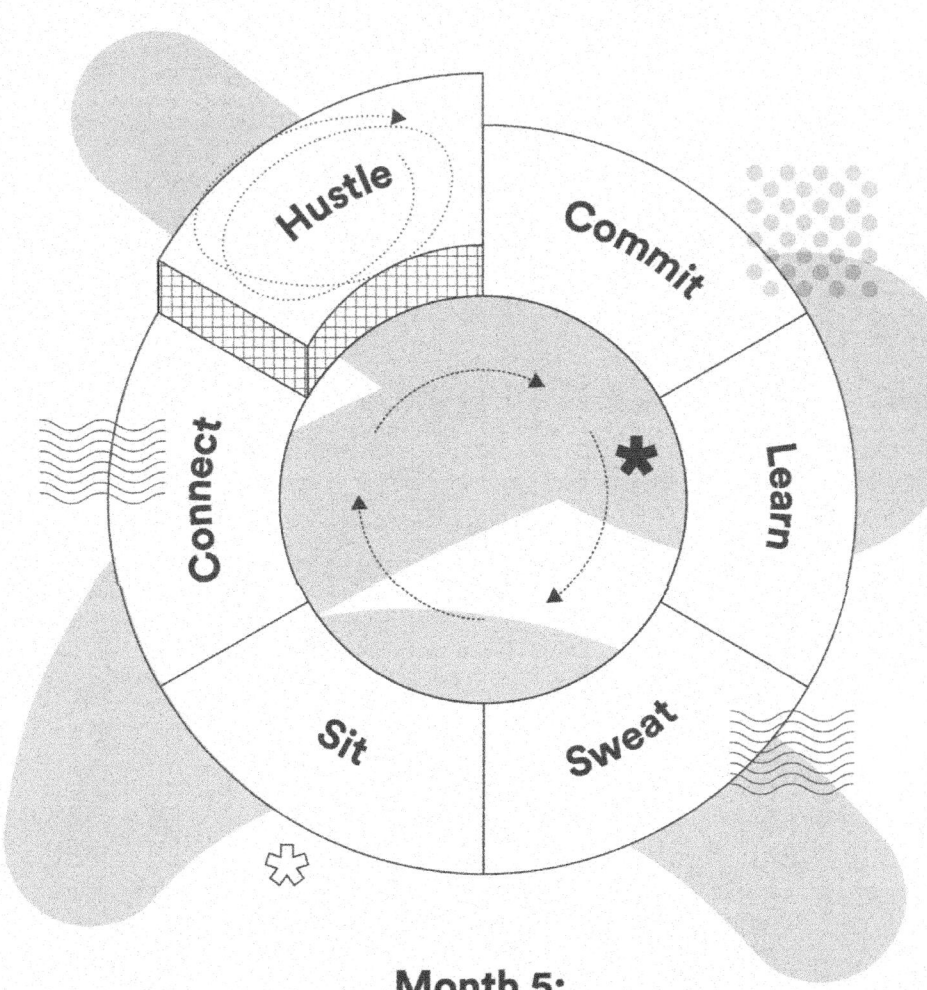

Month 5:
Hustle
Do your most important work for 30 minutes

CHAPTER 11

A DAY IN THE LIFE WITH THE SOBERPOWER METHOD

"The key to lifelong success is to make the decision, not to hope or think 'would,' 'should' or 'could' but know for certain that you will never drink again. If you hope you are going on holiday, it doesn't mean you are going anywhere, but if you know for certain, then you will definitely go. Once you make a firm decision, you cut off any other possibility and doubt; so whatever happens in your future life, drinking alcohol is just not an option but something that you have no interest in doing. You have moved on and are free." (Jason Vale, Kick the Drink . . . Easily)

So what else is there to achieve and maintain sobriety? What else must you do to alter the course of your life? The answer is nothing. You now have everything you need in order to get your own SoberPowers. As I've said, getting sober is not easy, but it is not complicated either. The goal of the SoberPower Method is to help you turn your life around in a positive way by creating healthy routines and habits. It's a meaningful experience, and one that you can be truly excited about. Beyond that, it's about making yourself mentally, physically, and spiritually healthier than ever before. The SoberPower Method is all about taking control of your life and working to become the best version of yourself. That way, you make yourself better, and you make the world around you better. Once you are on this path, I think you'll feel the same way about booze that I do. That it's worthless poison, and that it did nothing for me. *I've given up absolutely nothing by getting sober.* Every area of my life has improved. Because of this, I know in my heart that getting sober was the best decision I've ever made, and I wouldn't go back for anything or anyone. I've enjoyed every minute of this journey, and I think you will too.

So please join me in saying "yes" to living with SoberPowers. Here's a summary of the process to reinforce these ideas and help you get started.

DAY 1: Commit - to sobriety and working your SoberPractice

First, you have to commit to being sober. Meaning that during the next five months, you will not be drinking. You will get to see what it's like to choose sobriety, and you'll enjoy all the benefits that come with that decision. If you don't like what you see after five months, you can always go back to your old ways or find a different approach.

Next, you have to take it a step further. You have to commit to working your SoberPractice. Remember, this isn't just about sobriety. You will reserve an hour of each day to enjoy solitude and do the bulk of your SoberPractice work. If you can manage to schedule this in the morning, I recommend it, as it will pay dividends throughout the day. If mornings will not work for you, pick any time of day that does. The thinking here is to build the routine of putting your health and well-being first. That's what successful people do, and our aim is to be one of them.

Change is all about habits. It takes time to successfully load habits so that they become automatic. So the next five months will be your habit loading phase. You'll get used to sobriety, putting yourself first, and all five habits of the SoberPractice. Any less time than that and you haven't given yourself, or this method, a fair shot.

Once you are committed, you will get started on your SoberPractice right away. This is how you'll move beyond sobriety and into living your best life. You'll go from being simply sober, to being a healthy and mission-driven person. You'll achieve this through working on all five parts of the SoberPractice: Learn, Sweat, Sit, Connect, and Hustle. You will focus on one area per month. Meaning you will load one habit per month. And you will move through the five areas in order, so that by the end of month five, you've gained all your SoberPowers.

MONTH 1: Learn - Read Kick the Drink for 20 minutes

The first part of the SoberPractice is to Learn. You will learn the truth about alcohol addiction and our cultural values by reading *Kick the Drink . . . Easily*. You will see past the brainwashing and lies. This will change your mind regarding what it means to drink alcohol and what it means to be sober. You will no longer feel as if you're being deprived of some beneficial substance. You will no longer feel like an alcoholic with no hope for a normal life. Instead, you will feel joyous about stepping off the dangerous roller coaster ride of alcohol addiction.

MONTH 2: Sweat - Exercise for 30 minutes

Next, it's time to Sweat. It's time to repair, and build, your body. You will do this through daily exercise that will make you physically strong and mentally focused. Say hello to all those endorphins! On top exercising, eating healthy and getting plenty of sleep are recommended for regaining your health and energy. All of these are straightforward habits that individually would change your life. Taken together, they will make you *unstoppable*. You will also be filled with confidence as your body heals and appearance improves. Pretty soon, you will feel so good, you'll wonder why you ever drank in the first place.

MONTH 3: Sit - Meditate for 15 minutes

The belief that you need a drug to cope with life needs be replaced with feelings of gratitude and acceptance. This won't happen automatically. It takes a lot of practice. And you will do just that through meditation, journaling, or prayer. In this way, you will find peace in the present moment. By finally taking the time to Sit, you will start to feel good about your current situation and see it as an opportunity to make your life great.

MONTH 4: Connect - Call a friend for 10 minutes

It's time to rejoin the world again. It's time to Connect. During the fourth month of your SoberPractice, you'll build a solid social foundation by connecting openly with positive people. Nobody does this alone, and sharing your life with your loved ones is one of the greatest gifts of being sober. As your relationships improve, so will your emotional life.

MONTH 5: Hustle - Do your most important work for 30 minutes

The last part of the SoberPractice is to Hustle. At this time, you'll turn your attention away from yourself. And you'll start pursuing your passions and life mission. This is also known as your most important work. You will answer the following questions:

- What am I good at?

- What do I enjoy doing?

- What can I do to benefit others?

As you start working on these things, you will notice improvements in your focus and mental clarity. You will feel amazing knowing that you are no longer squandering your life—you are using it to make the world a better place.

And that's it. For five months, you'll follow this SoberPractice of growth and self-discovery. The goal is to get you sober *and* living your best life. That way, there will be no regrets or shame. Only positive growth and the sense of appreciation that comes with it. That is how you're going to turn your life around.

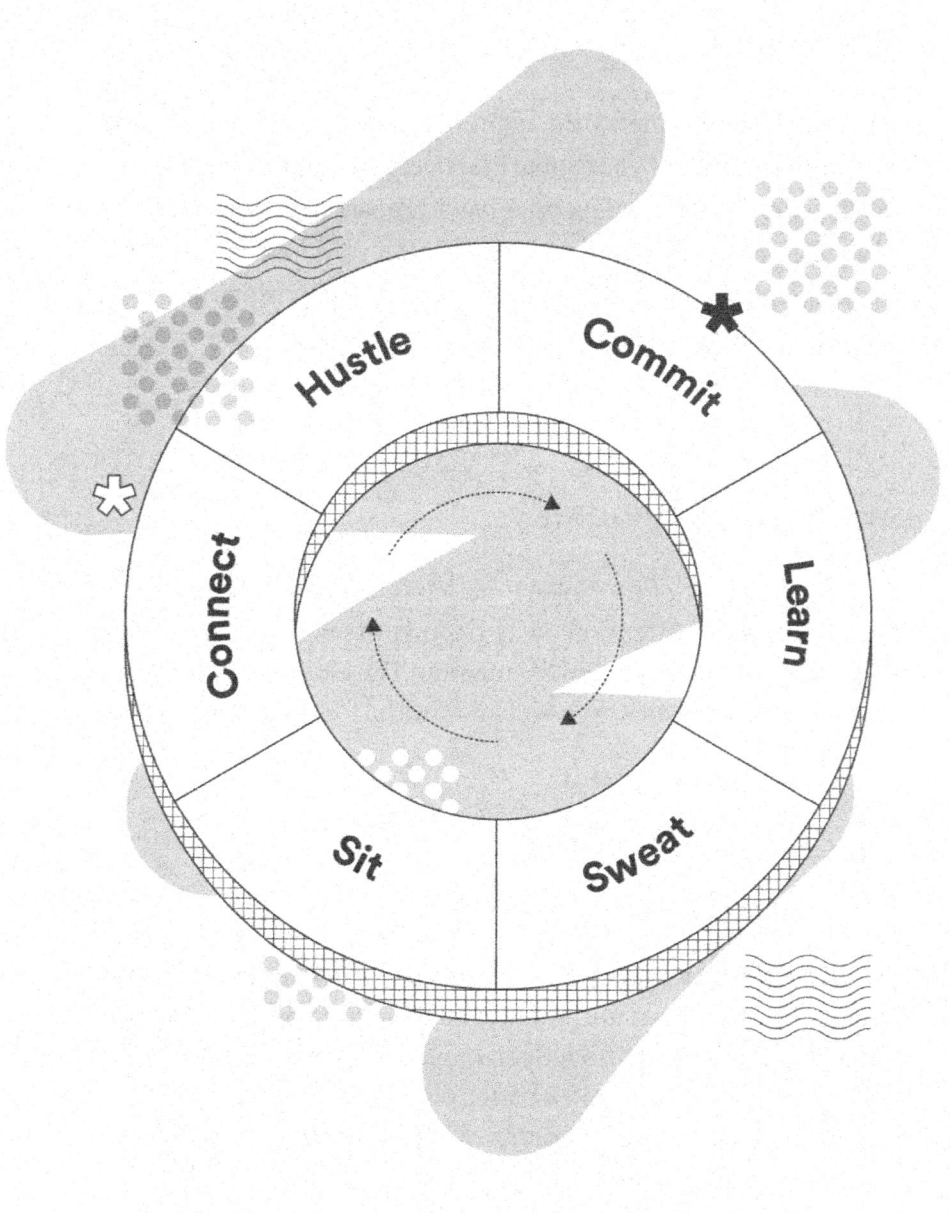

A Day in the Life

To conclude this chapter, I want to show you an example of what your SoberPractice may look like on a given day. As I've said, it's not about doing as much as you can in a day. It's about consistently doing something every day so that it becomes a habit.

Below is an example of my own SoberPractice. If you were thinking I quit working my SoberPractice, since I'm two years sober, you'd be wrong. I don't really think about alcohol much anymore, but the habits I've built will stick with me for life. I truly enjoy this. It's what fires me up every morning when I get out of bed. Like I keep saying, the SoberPower Method is not just about being sober. It's about living your best life, and my SoberPractice enables me to do just that. It's evolved over the past two years, as will yours, but it still has me on the road of continuous self-improvement. I can't ask for much more than that.

As you read about my daily work below, keep in mind that I have loaded all five of the SoberPractice habits. So this is what your SoberPractice may look like at the end of month five. But for the first few months, it's much simpler as you build up each habit individually and incrementally. Once you get to the end of month five, you're going to feel so good that maintaining all these habits is second nature.

- 6:00 AM: I wake up early, with energy and focus, to work on myself. There are no distractions or interruptions at this hour. I meditate and read for 15 minutes each. In the early days, I read *Kick the Drink* and other sobriety-related books. Today, I have moved on to other subjects that interest me. To this day, this quiet time fills me with peace. And that's something I will always need to replenish and renew. After meditating and reading, I do my most important work for the next hour. That includes following all of my deepest passions and goals. This fills me with intention and purpose, as I'm doing work aligned with my ultimate mission. All combined, this takes an hour and a half of my day. People don't believe me, but it's by far my favorite time. Not only do I get a lot of high quality work done, but it fuels the rest of my day. I feel unstoppable by the time I walk out the door to head to work.

- 2:00 PM: I go to the gym for an hour to follow my CrossFit program. Like I said, I have to be ready for anything. I train in the gym during the work week only. On weekends, I either do something outside, such as golfing or biking, or I rest my body.

- 6:00 PM: After work, I try to do something social with my friends or girlfriend. If I don't hang out with someone face-to-face, I'll call a friend who lives out of town. This takes anywhere from 15 minutes to an entire evening. Once again, this isn't a chore at all.

- 10:00 PM: I go to bed so that I will get eight hours of sleep before my SoberPractice starts back up the next day. This doesn't take time, either. It just takes discipline to make sleep a priority and build healthy habits around that. Despite how much more productive I am as a sober person, I feel infinitely more rested than ever before. Just another reason to get sober, right?

I bet you can see that my SoberPractice is not complicated or time consuming. It's pretty normal, right? But most people aren't able to commit to normal and healthy habits. Most people get in their own way, and I used to be one of them. Those days are long gone. My above daily routine is just me living my best life, which is actually pretty normal at this point.

And it's not like I have a stopwatch out counting the seconds. I enjoy all the habits I've formed, and wish I had even more time for my SoberPractice. All said, it's an hour or so of quiet time in the morning, an hour of fitness in the afternoon, and some time spent with loved ones during the evening. Beyond that, it's a handful of healthy and productive decisions sprinkled throughout the day, such as eating healthy food and getting to bed on time. As I keep saying, this isn't rocket science. Neither is getting sober. It's a simple life lived intentionally, rather than chasing the fleeting pleasure of another dopamine fix. These habits are fundamental and would work for anyone wanting to recover from trauma or addiction. And for anyone wanting to grow and improve.

The Maintenance Phase

After five months of following your SoberPractice, you will have successfully navigated the habit loading phase, and with that, you'll have a set of truly life-changing habits. You'll have built these gradually, so that you could fully dedicate your willpower to one habit at a time. This is the most efficient way I know to create lasting change both inside and outside yourself. At the end of five months, you will feel great about yourself and your new path forward.

Then you enter the second (and last) phase of habit building. The maintenance phase. What this means is that your habits are just that—habits. As simple as the SoberPractice is, it's even easier when you are in the maintenance phase. I don't even think about getting up early to meditate anymore. In fact, it feels weird if it doesn't happen. And making healthy eating decisions doesn't take much effort either. I've witnessed firsthand how much better I feel when I eat real food, so the decision practically makes itself. And it's the same with sobriety. For the first couple months, it was weird turning down drinks and being the sober one in the group. But that feeling has changed now. I've gotten used to it, and like all the other SoberPractice habits, I love the feeling I get from consciously choosing sobriety.

Having these healthy habits fully ingrained is the final SoberPower, because once you actually enjoy being on this path, there is little chance of you ever straying from it. That's why I don't count my days of sobriety anymore. There is no destination— only growth. I just follow my SoberPractice every day, and that's enough for me. That's living with SoberPowers.

CHAPTER 12

THE SOBERCHARGED LIFE

=======================================

"One of the biggest joys of being free is the sudden realisation that everything we will ever need is within us already. We have the ability to meet every challenge. We have the courage to overcome any fears. We have the capability to feel joy and happiness at a moment's notice. We have the finest drug in the world in its purest form already within us and it's free of charge. It is called the life force. It is the buzz we get from being alive, growing every day and embracing new opportunities." (Jason Vale, Kick the Drink . . . Easily!)

I want to leave you with a final message. At all times, please remember that your new SoberPower habits and lifestyle are the start of something amazing. Two years ago, when I was still stuck in the trap of alcohol addiction, the thought of becoming sober seemed impossible. It filled me with fear. I didn't know anyone who didn't drink, and I couldn't imagine life without alcohol. Then I went to treatment and was filled with discouragement and shame. AA meetings weren't much better. I didn't want to live a life dominated by meetings and living in the past. I didn't want to be branded as an alcoholic for the rest of my days. I didn't want to be weird. I met many people who followed AA religiously. That lifestyle worked for a few of them, but it was obvious to me that I would never fit in. Honestly, I was stuck, and I didn't know where to turn. I just knew I had to do something.

So I started working on myself. I read *Kick the Drink*, and found out that everything I thought I knew about drinking and sobriety was bullshit. I started working out more often, and found out that having a healthy lifestyle was a hell of a lot more fun than being hungover and overweight. I connected with family and friends, and learned that I liked the sober and clear-headed version of myself much more than the *creepy drunk guy* I'd been all those years. I started meditating regularly, and discovered that peace and joy cannot be found in a bottle. It has to come from within.

So yeah, I pursued self-improvement in every possible way, and in the process, I got sober. I completely flipped both my mind-set and lifestyle, and I loved every minute of it. This is how I developed the SoberPower Method - stuck in a seemingly lose-lose situation and desperate to claw my way out. But it became more than the way out of my self-imposed predicament. It became my way forward as well. Now, I invite you on the SoberPower journey. It can become your way forward too.

One Last Reminder

Let me give you one final recap. The primary work of the SoberPower Method is to load and adopt a set of healthy and productive habits. These habits are performed daily, becoming your SoberPractice. You will follow this for at least five months, so that these habits become an enjoyable and easy part of your lifestyle. You will evolve as a person. Instead of utilizing will-power to stay sober, you will eliminate any desire to drink. This is the core principle of the SoberPower Method. It's change, not through willpower and discipline, but through personal growth and evolution.

You won't even feel regret or shame about the time you spent drinking. Instead, you will come to accept your old ways as a necessary mistake. A mistake you're grateful you made and thank-ful you've moved on from. You will not envy other drinkers. You will actually feel sorry for them, and realize that they will never have the same quality of life as you. On top of all of that, you will be improving in all areas of your life. After Committing, you will Learn, Sweat, Sit, Connect, and Hustle. You will focus on each area, one month at a time, in that order. You will truly feel blessed to have found your new life direction. You'll realize that getting sober doesn't need to be complicated, and there is no reason to get down on yourself. Focus on today's SoberPractice only, and the rest of your life will take care of itself.

In time, I think you'll agree that your new SoberPowered life is as different from your drinking days as a dream is from a nightmare. I still marvel at all the changes I've made. Before getting sober, I could barely hold a job. My relationships were falling apart. I was overweight. I lived in constant fear. Yet, for some reason, I thought this was normal. I somehow thought that alcohol was providing me with a genuine benefit. It clearly wasn't. I was merely brainwashed. I see the truth now, and I don't recognize that line of thinking anymore. I wouldn't go back for any amount of money.

It is my hope that this book fills you with excitement for your five months ahead. There is truly nothing better than waking up with a clear head, a healthy body, and the confident desire to move forward with your life. That said, you should know that this initial excitement could wear off the same way the newness wears off in a romantic relationship. When it does, your habits and personal convictions should be strong enough to keep you going. Some people call this initial euphoria the "pink cloud effect." Don't worry about this. It's completely normal and actually just shows that you are leveling up. Again, if your excitement does decrease a little bit, it has still served its purpose in getting you motivated at the start. After that, your habits will take over, and you can get to the real work of using your SoberPowers to pursue self-growth. And then you get to be excited about something else.

A Look at the Path Ahead

The SoberPower Method isn't just about getting you out of the trap of alcohol addiction. It's about putting you on the path to a great life. It's about finding your way and starting your own SoberPower journey. Call it what you will, but you won't find true peace and joy until you are living authentically and following your true calling in life. By working your SoberPractice, you are taking the first steps, and you will realize that the only thing alcohol did was hold you back. You will learn a lot about yourself during the quiet mornings following your SoberPractice. And as you are living in the moment and treating yourself right, you will be buzzing with energy throughout the day.

This is where I am today. I rarely think about alcohol anymore. Instead, I think about my purpose and what I can do to move things forward every day. I think about improving myself, so that I can be of help to others. I think about creating something that will benefit the world and leave behind a legacy. I think about building up those around me and having an amazing social circle. That's where I'm at right now, and going back to the days of drinking and not moving any of these things forward seems like suicide. That's why I'm asking you to join me in committing to the SoberPower lifestyle. It's time to get your SoberPowers. Today.

What have you got to lose?

CHAPTER 13

APPENDIX

PUTTING YOUR POWERS
TO PRACTICE

You now understand how to achieve sobriety through the SoberPower Method. Hopefully, you're ready to commit to sobriety and your own SoberPractice. Regardless of where you are at, you can probably guess that your life is about to be completely different. This is a good thing and something to be excited about. But there are two things you have to remember.

The first is that you are beginning the process of changing your lifestyle, habits, and possibly even your values. I am not here to tell you what to think or who to be, but I can guarantee that you will not be the same person you were as a drinker. Change happens when you beat an addiction, meditate, learn new things, and work on yourself every day. From this change in values and priorities will come new ideas about how to live your life and achieve lasting success. The following chapters will impart some of the major revelations that I've had during the past two years of living with SoberPowers. These things may not be entirely true for you, but I hope that they can help guide you in the coming months. Maybe serve a little bit like a field manual. You will also have your own insights during this time that will serve as your guide going forward.

The second thing to note is that there will be many challenges ahead. Prioritizing your SoberPractice will go a long way in helping you get over these hurdles. But most of that work is done on your own, most likely during peaceful morning hours. The real world usually isn't as forgiving or understanding. Remember, people in the real world are brainwashed. One of the most difficult parts of the SoberPower Method is maintaining your positive mindset during difficult situations and among challenging people. The following chapters will outline some of these difficult situations, and how I have successfully navigated them.

DISEASE OR BAD HABIT?

I'm not in recovery, and I don't have a drinking problem. Let me repeat—I'm not in recovery, and I don't have a drinking problem. Want another example of brainwashing? Most people (both sober and not) refer to alcohol addiction as a disease. Some of them say you will have this "disease" for the rest of your life, and that you are simply in remission if you are able to cut out the booze. Others believe that you are "cured" when you stop drinking.

Well, to be honest, I just don't believe any of it. From my experiences drinking every day, to finally overcoming that desire, I believe alcohol addiction is simply a bad habit that gets out of control. To be certain, alcoholism is one of the worst habits you can have, weakening your mind, body, and spirit. Alcohol also stupefies you, so that it is very difficult to see the trap you are walking into. But I don't think the past two years have been me getting over a disease. It just doesn't feel like that at all. I think it has been me working hard to overcome a bad habit that had the potential to ruin my life or kill me.

"But they say your brain changes. Doesn't that make it more than a bad habit?"

Actually, no, it doesn't. The truth is, our brains change when we establish just about any habit. It even changes when we learn something new. Your brain is always changing. Whether you are learning a new skill, reading a book, or eating dinner, your brain and body are in constant motion. It's called neuroplasticity, and it's normal. It's not a disease.

"Why does it matter, anyway?"

Because, in my opinion, believing yourself to have an incurable lifelong disease is not a productive mindset to have. It breeds fear and uncertainty regarding your present situation and future outlook. Because if you go through life thinking you have a disease that could come back to bite you at any time, you might end up playing the victim card and refusing to take action when you need it the most. I've seen this happen to people firsthand.

So no, I don't think I've healed from a disease. I believe I've overcome my own weaknesses —something I will continue to do in various ways for the rest of my life.

A Lifetime of Recovery

Speaking of the rest of my life, many ex-drinkers use the term "recovery" when referring to their lives after drinking. I don't do this either. That word doesn't apply to my current mindset at all. As a matter of experience, it just doesn't make sense.

Sure, I think some recovery takes place during the first weeks and months after stopping drinking. Your body and mind have been sick for years. It takes some time to bounce back. But once you've kicked the drinking habit, followed your SoberPractice, and moved on freely, you are no longer in recovery. You are living a healthy and worthwhile life.

Once again, the devil is in the details. Recovery is a negative word implying that we're still healing from something. Does it really take the rest of our lives to do that? Are we still recovering when alcohol is out of our system, we have no interest whatsoever in drinking, and our lives are better than ever? I don't think so, and I sure as hell don't want to tell people I'm recovering for the rest of my days. I couldn't be any happier as a sober person, and my drinking days just feel like a bad dream at this point anyway. I will not allow my past to define me for the rest of my life.

Living a life in recovery implies that we're spending our time trying to get back to some vague definition of normal. This is not how I see my life. I got back to normal a long time ago, and now I'm striving to be a better person than I was before I had my first sip of alcohol.

My Drinking Problem

One last term that gets thrown around, by both drinkers and non-drinkers alike, is "drinking problem." According to many brainwashed people, I currently have a drinking problem. Yes, two years sober, and I still have a problem. What's with all the negativity? How do I have a drinking problem when I no longer drink or have any desire to do so? Alcohol plays zero role in my life, so how do I still have a problem with it?

It's not me who has a drinking problem. It's the people who still think there is something to be gained by drinking who have drinking problems. And I mean that in the most respectful and compassionate way. But it's true. Even the most minor of drinkers has more of a drinking problem than I have at this point. I can't count the number of normies I've had to forgive for their hangovers during the past two years. I count myself blessed not to have this *problem* anymore.

To be fair, I know that I was never able to control my alcohol intake in the past, and it's highly unlikely I would be able to do so in the future if I made the stupid decision to drink again. So in this way, I agree that a certain part of my general makeup may be predisposed to alcohol addiction. If I started drinking again, yes, I would have a minor drinking problem that would more than likely escalate into a major one. I accept this about myself at this point, but I also know that that day will never come. I no longer believe in the benefits of alcohol, and I have left the drinking problem behind with everything else.

So to answer my original question, no, I do not have a drinking problem, and I am not recovering from a disease. I used to have a very bad habit in the form of a drinking problem. I'll admit that I was addicted, and nobody knows better than me that alcohol can take over your life. But I replaced that drinking habit with my SoberPractice. That's what gets me out of bed now. It took a few months to recover from all the crap that went down inside and around me, but I did just that. I healed, moved on, and am now free. I don't have a drinking problem because I don't drink. And there is nothing left to recover from.

LOVE THE STRUGGLE

One of the biggest pitfalls of modern society is our insistence on chasing pleasure. Whether it's buying the new toy, watching the latest show on Netflix, or meeting that special someone, we are constantly exposed to happy people achieving some mysterious form of lasting pleasure. An external form of pleasure that is found outside oneself. If you didn't know any better, you'd think this was the goal of life: to be entertained, to be comfortable, and to feel good.

It's no different with alcohol and drug use. From a marketing perspective, drinking is broadcast to us as a genuine pleasure. Something worth having at the end of a stressful day and something necessary to live the good life. We've all seen the commercials with the attractive group of friends, dressed to impress, all assembled at the bar and ready to take their first sip of the evening. Alcohol companies are smart. They make drinking look relaxing and sophisticated.

On a personal level, that is exactly what we are looking for when we drink. We want to forget about the day. We want to relax and settle into a more carefree mindset. We want some pleasure.

But even people without SoberPowers know that drinking doesn't work like this. Any momentary pleasure you get from alcohol doesn't last very long. And even during the brief period of time that it does, what is it really doing for you? Is a life of worry-free pleasure really the goal?

The very short answer is "no." Life isn't about attaining pleasure. Not for those of us with a growth mindset anyway. That's because, by definition, pleasure is fleeting and does not last.

How long were you happy after you bought that new car? How satisfied were you after you finished your 27th series on Netflix? Taking it even further, how happy were you when you lost that ten pounds? What about when you got that raise at work?

I'm sure you were happy for a certain period of time, and that's not a bad thing. But the feeling of satisfaction faded, right? The problem with external happiness is that it does not last, and when it goes away, you just want more. Something else. So you grasp and look for your next fix. Pleasure is fleeting by nature, so to define yourself by it, is to deny yourself lasting joy and peace.

What Will Drive Your Life?

So what should we be aiming for instead? What is the goal? As I've said, it's not temporary pleasure or achievement. Pleasure is kind of like dessert. It's something nice to enjoy after dinner, but it's not the focal point of the meal. Pleasure is more like a fancy decoration than the foundation of your house. It's nice to have, but it's not the reason your house is standing.

Instead, what we should be looking for is lasting joy. And the only place you'll find it is in the struggle. True happiness lies in the process. We must enjoy the daily work, our SoberPractice, because the process is all about what's inside of you. It's the work you put into yourself. It's also the failures that go along with it.

If you need proof, just look around you. If you ask a self-made millionaire what makes her happy, is it ever the number in her bank account? Rarely. Typically, this successful person misses the days before she made that million dollars, when she was scrapping and hustling just to get by. More often than not, she is still waking up at dawn to scrap and hustle. Why? It's because she values the process that made her a success, not the rewards that came with it. Sure, those are nice, but they don't lead to lasting happiness, and they aren't worth living for.

On the other side of the spectrum, take the guy who made a million dollars winning the lottery. We've all read these types of sob stories. That million dollars led to family problems, an extravagant and spiritually hollow lifestyle, and to less happiness than he had before he "struck gold." This is because money will not make you happy. There was no struggle or process required for this person to become rich, so there was no lasting happiness when it happened. It's simply an empty achievement. It's a number in his bank account. And because this person didn't build the skills necessary to handle himself, or that type of money, he is likely left off worse than before he luckily became rich.

Find happiness in the struggle. Enjoy the process of getting up early every day for your SoberPractice. That's what the SoberPower Method is all about. It's not about some distant point in the future, when you haven't had a drink in ten years, and have the rest of your life sorted out. It's about *now*. It's about how shitty you feel *now*, and how you are going to get your SoberPractice going anyway—*now*.

If you are like I was two years ago, this is the struggle in which you currently find yourself. Enjoy the monotony of meditating every morning. Learn to love the bad days in the gym when you feel sluggish. This is the process that you will come to enjoy more than the rewards it will undoubtedly bring. And to be honest, it wouldn't surprise me if one day you look upon this time the same way that self-made millionaire looks upon her early years grinding. You might miss the struggle when things weren't as easy. I sure do. Because now you have nothing to lose, and you are building yourself up. Enjoy this time. Enjoy every time. Learn to love the struggle, and you will find everlasting joy.

BEING SOCIAL
WITHOUT ALCOHOL

During the past two years, I've had a lot of time to reflect on what my reasons were for drinking in the first place. I know why it got bad. It was a combination of my breakup, the deeply ingrained habit of using alcohol as a crutch, and the addictive characteristics of the substance itself. But why did someone like me, healthy and from a good family, start drinking to excess in the first place? Like all addictions, there were a variety of reasons, but I think the most important for me was social anxiety.

Although most people these days would probably never guess, I've suffered from a lack of social confidence going back about as far as I can remember. Not all the time. It's very situational for me. But it's something I've dealt with nonetheless, and it seemed to get worse as I entered adulthood. I was always fine going to work or being with good friends, but put me in a difficult situation, a first date or a bar filled with strangers, and I felt like a totally different person. Since then, I've learned that these feelings, in moderation, are completely normal, but experiencing social anxiety sucks nonetheless.

As most people know, one of the most common remedies for social anxiety is, you guessed it, alcohol. It's why alcohol is referred to as a "social lubricant" and why it's guzzled down like water at weddings, work parties, and just about everywhere else. People drink because it makes them feel more open and comfortable around other people. It eases their nerves and numbs their fear. Drinking can turn a boring party into an energetic one and an awkward silence into conversation. Sometimes, it's almost as if alcohol is the life of the party, and not the people who are drinking it.

Conquering the Fear of Not Being Enough

One of the biggest fears I had when I got sober was how I would handle social situations without booze. Addiction is all about acting on emotional triggers until the response becomes a habit. For me, the simple act of meeting up with friends was a reason to drink. Because of this, in almost any social situation, I drank. This continued for years until it became a habit. Anytime I went out, my first thought would be whether or not there would be enough alcohol to satisfy me for the evening.

Outside influences only confirmed to me that it was perfectly normal to drink at social events. I work at a company with a heavy drinking culture. At just about any team celebration, alcohol is handed out like it's spring break. And then outside of work, you got the happy hours, sporting events, and concerts. At just about any function in this country where people come together, alcohol plays a major role. Not only that, but sometimes it seems to play the primary role, while the purported reason for being there takes a back seat.

And then there were dates. There was absolutely no way I was meeting up with women if booze wasn't involved. I couldn't have imagined presenting myself confidently, to someone I didn't know, without alcohol in those days. So yes, I drank to excess at every date. Hell, I even drank before dates to ease my nerves. Needless to say, I don't really know who the person was I was presenting to others back then.

What all this boils down to is that drinking played a major role in my social life a few years ago. When my life started to fall apart and I considered quitting, I couldn't imagine having any type of exciting social life without alcohol. I figured I was done for. That I was destined for a life sitting at the kids' table on the rare occasions that I wasn't at an AA meeting. Not only that, but I figured that when I did venture out to meet new people, I'd have to deal with my social anxiety head on, without a single coping mechanism. Sounds fun, huh?

Walking Without a Crutch

Well, I haven't drank alcohol in over two years, and as I've said throughout this book, I do not miss it at all. Though quite different, my social life is actually *better* than it was during my drinking days. There are fewer foggy nights at the bar and more healthy activities outdoors. Now, when I do go out, it's to hear music I like or to meet up with people I enjoy. I'm not there for the tap list.

I've described many benefits of sobriety throughout this book. Not waking up with anxiety and hangovers is game-changing. Having the mental and physical energy to pursue my SoberPractice is massive. But not being the guy with a drink in my hand at all times is just as amazing. Because drinking all the time meant it was controlling me. Having to drink during social events was not only taking a toll on my health, it was decreasing my freedom. I truly was a slave to alcohol.

I wouldn't say my social anxiety has gone away entirely, but contrary to what I believed, it's dramatically less than it was when

I was drinking. I repeat, by removing the crutch I had for dealing with nerve-racking social situations, I have made them much less scary. This is because drinking wasn't improving me in any way. It was merely enabling me to avoid my issues. I wasn't growing in confidence or improving my social skills. I wasn't learning from my experiences, as I couldn't remember most of them. Drinking didn't solve any of my problems. It just numbed the pain caused by not dealing with them.

But now, I'm free. The Band-Aid has been ripped off. I don't hide behind a mask of drunkenness when I go out and socialize with people. It's just me, all the time. I'm fully present to work on my social skills and face the social anxiety head on. All of this has happened naturally. And my confidence has skyrocketed simply through knowing that I no longer need alcohol. When I first got sober, I imagined that my social life would take a dramatic hit. In fact, it's been the complete opposite. There are ironies and surprises hidden throughout the SoberPower journey, but they are *real*. I've never felt better spending time with other people.

So what have I learned that has helped me to move on from my socially anxious past? As I've mentioned throughout this book, it's simply that the key to feeling comfortable around others is the willingness to be open and vulnerable. And to face your fears head on. I used to think that I needed to drink and act cool to be accepted. I've been through a lot during the past two years, and the more open I am with others about myself and my story, the better I connect with them. Sunshine truly is the best disinfectant.

By telling others about my fears and weaknesses, I've inspired them to do the same. Instead of looking down on me, my friends admire the courage that I have to be comfortable in my own skin, on my own terms, and without alcohol. Once again, it's the opposite of what I expected. Who would have thought that being sober and open was the answer to a fun and rewarding social life?

DEALING WITH PEOPLE WHO DRINK

Hopefully, you are now convinced that committing to the SoberPower lifestyle will be worth it for you. It's the most significant step towards self-improvement that I have found. It beats any juice cleanse, self-help book, or life hack on the market. You are finally going to stop consuming an addictive poison. What could possibly be better than that?

Although the SoberPower Method provides amazing benefits in both the short and long term, there are certainly struggles along the way. Not everything about life after drinking is easy. For one thing, you are about to be a social outlier. And trust me, I mean that in a positive way. You don't want to be just another drinker.

Let's face it—the average person in our society drinks alcohol. Most people drink it regularly. Many people drink it to excess. That's because it's one of the few drugs in our society that is widely accepted and promoted. Even with SoberPowers, this is the environment and culture you will be living in. You are going to feel different when you go out. You may even feel a bit awkward at times. You will see, however, that this is no reason to get down on yourself or doubt your decision. In fact, it's a reason to celebrate your commitment and remind yourself how far you've come.

But still, it's not easy in the beginning. I've been in countless situations where I felt awkward as hell not drinking. Once, I was with 30+ co-workers who were all taking a shot of tequila to toast a member of our team who passed away. All eyes were on me as the tray of shot glasses was passed around. People were already tipsy, and there was anticipation in the air. Needless to say, I stuck with my glass of sparkling water in a situation where it almost seemed rude. I just smiled and passed the tray to the next guy. I work closely with these people, and a few of them know that I no longer drink. It was probably obvious to quite a few people what was going on. So yes, this was a bit uncomfortable. But the awkward feeling passed, and I left that bar feeling proud of myself. And coherent. I don't know if too many others could have said the same.

Two Roads Diverged

I've gone to dinners and been on dates during the past two years at which it genuinely shocks people when I order a non-alcoholic drink. Sometimes, I'm even asked directly why I'm not drinking. Maybe they think nothing of it. But maybe they are making assumptions about me. I've been to family reunions, music festivals, alcohol-fueled work dinners, and travelled across the world since I quit drinking. I've been thrown in just about any situation you can imagine. Situations in which my old self would have reached for a drink. But I haven't wavered. And equipped with SoberPowers, it hasn't really been that difficult.

So yeah, choosing sobriety is taking the road less travelled. Be prepared for it. But in the end, who cares? I'm living with SoberPowers. I'm constantly growing and improving myself. I live in the moment, and I no longer need a drug to avoid challenges or struggles. I accept those challenges and find ways to solve them. And that goes for hanging out with other people as well. I don't need to drink to enjoy myself, and I will no longer suffer the following day because I had a good time.

Although making the more popular decision, drinkers cannot say any of these things. They still habitually use a drug in order to relax around other people. Most likely, they won't be waking up the next morning clear headed and energized to work on themselves. I'm not saying everyone drinks to the extent that I did, as some people clearly have quite a bit of control, but it is doubtful they are on the same path of self-improvement that I am. So what's so bad about taking the road less travelled?

The truth is, I feel a little bit sorry for drinkers these days. Sometimes it's funny to see them let loose and make fools of themselves. But it's truly a pity to be a slave to a drug that provides no benefits. Being sober in a room full of drinkers has only confirmed this to me. I cannot count the number of times people have confided in me that they wished they drank less or that they were envious of my lifestyle. Or all the times I've witnessed completely normal people do regrettable things while under the influence. Yeah, I don't miss that either.

I don't mean to say that I look down on drinkers. How could I? I did these very same things for the majority of my life. It's just that I couldn't be happier to be done with that way of life—sober. Far from feeling jealous, I am relieved and grateful to be off of the roller coaster. When the next day rolls around, and I can still get up early with a clear memory of the night before, I feel like I've unlocked some sort of cheat code on how to live the good life.

So be happy with your decision to be sober. Celebrate it, even when you are out with others, and there isn't a crutch in sight. The decision to quit drinking will literally mark a new season of your life. Use your time around others to remind yourself how good it is to be living with SoberPowers.

REHAB AND PHARMACEUTICALS

After reading this book and learning about my experience getting sober, you may be thinking,

"Drew, the SoberPower Method is all well and good, but didn't you go to rehab? How do you know that your time and learnings there were not what kept you sober, instead of all of this SoberPractice stuff?"

That's a good question and something I've given a lot of thought to. To be clear, I spent three weeks in rehab and have gone through two outpatient programs. I learned a lot at each of these stops and met some great people. To be honest, it's impossible to completely separate this formalized treatment from my *earliest* SoberPractice work. At the time, I was desperate to find a way out of my addictive lifestyle. All of the work I did, both formal and on my own, was one big push towards sobriety.

If I'm being honest, treatment was good for me. It gave me a break from my bad habits. It allowed me to detox from all the poison I was putting into my body. And it was clear evidence that I was at rock bottom. Sure, I could have probably gone even further into the abyss of addiction, but being forced to leave work to go to rehab with other drug addicts was not a place I thought I'd ever find myself. Because of all these things, treatment opened my mind. I couldn't ignore my issues anymore. As I felt the alcohol leave my body, I knew that it should have never been there in the first place. I had to find a new way of life.

So it's in this way that rehab actually led to the SoberPower Method. As I've mentioned previously, my counselors predominantly advocated AA's approach to recovery. I knew that wouldn't work for me, but I did have to find a way. I had to do something, and at rehab, I had plenty of free time to do it. So I started my SoberPractice during my stay at treatment, and I haven't looked back since.

Formalized Treatment as a Viable Option

I don't think treatment is a bad option. If you are finding it impossible to quit drinking (the first step of the SoberPower Method), or your addiction is seriously damaging your life, it's probably right for you. Like I said, it's a great opportunity to take a break from your normal responsibilities, detox from alcohol, and open your mind to new ideas. It's a great place to begin your SoberPractice.

But if you are excited to choose sobriety and fired up to start your SoberPractice, treatment may not be necessary for you. Regardless of what you choose, I recommend starting your SoberPractice, on your own or at treatment, the day you commit to sobriety.

Naltrexone as a Viable Option

Regarding pharmaceutical drugs, please know that these next few paragraphs simply reflect my personal opinions. I'm not a medical professional. This is not medical advice. I'm also required, by law, to suggest that you seek the advice of a doctor before making any decisions about which drugs to use for yourself.

That said, another tool I'm not against employing is a pharmaceutical drug called Naltrexone. This once-a-day pill can help ease any cravings you may experience during your first couple months of sobriety. It would also weaken the effects of alcohol if you were to drink, serving as a sort of lifeline if you were to slip-up. Basically, if you were to drink on Naltrexone, you wouldn't feel much at all. This could make that slip-up much less damaging, allowing you to move on with your SoberPower journey.

I used Naltrexone for the first couple months after I got sober. It was given to me during treatment, and I figured that I should do everything in my power to stop drinking. It's impossible to say how much of an effect it had on me. Once I quit taking it after the first couple months, I didn't notice any changes at all. I was the same sober person with the same SoberPowered mindset. No cravings for alcohol emerged.

In my opinion, Naltrexone is a good option for those who are experiencing overpowering cravings for alcohol in the beginning of their SoberPower journey, or for those who may need a confidence boost to get started. Naltrexone is not a crutch. It's just another example of the commitment you are making to get sober. Sobriety is not easy in the beginning, and you should do everything in your power to make it work.

In the end, however, treatment and pharmaceuticals will only go so far. I met people in treatment who had been over ten times. I know people who have relapsed while on Naltrexone. I've seen people drink on days they were planning to go to their inpatient class. Truly, both rehab and Naltrexone are good tools, but you have to make the change *internally* if you want to live with SoberPowers. You have to want to be sober with all your soul. You have to Commit, Learn, Sweat, Sit, Connect, and Hustle. And you have to love the decision you are making.

So make the commitment now. Start your SoberPractice today, and if you think you need some additional support or medical advice, pursue formalized treatment or Naltrexone as well. It never hurts to have additional tools in your arsenal.

MANAGING YOUR MISTAKES

This is it. The final chapter. After this, it's all about you and your SoberPower journey. It will be your time to take action, kick your alcohol addiction, and get started on your own adventure. But I would be remiss if I didn't mention that, like all worthwhile undertakings, the SoberPower path is not always a smooth one.

Mistakes and temporary lapses can happen on this path, but this is no different than any other major life change where deeply ingrained habits are involved. You are making the best choice of your life, and it's not always going to be easy. As I've mentioned previously, there are going to be times where you are emotionally triggered to drink. Going to social events sober may not be easy at first. Dealing with stress head on, and without the crutch of alcohol, is probably new to you.

As such, you may fall off the path from time to time. Just remember that this is normal, and what matters is that you stay committed in the long term. Your SoberPractice progress is not negated by these mistakes and slip-ups. This work is cumulative, and will pick up right where you left off, if you are able to quickly recommit yourself to the SoberPower Method. You may even find yourself stronger going forward, as you learn from your mistakes, and are better able to handle yourself in the future.

For me, mistakes were definitely part of the process. Once I admitted to myself that I really needed to stop drinking, it took about eight months for me to actually do so. During this time, I waffled back and forth, drinking occasionally despite my near-rock-bottom circumstances. But I learned a lot. I went to outpatient classes. I read books. I reflected on what life without alcohol would mean to me. At the time, these eight months were horrible for both me and my loved ones. I wasn't really supposed to be drinking during this time, so it appeared to others as if I didn't care. It seemed like I would never be able to commit to sobriety.

But looking back on it now, I realize that those eight months were absolutely necessary for me to say yes to my SoberPower journey. It wasn't a rock bottom at all. Like I said, at the beginning of that time period, I finally admitted I had a problem with alcohol. My drinking bouts thereafter only confirmed this to me, and I *needed* this confirmation. I felt guilty every time I drank and learned what a worthless poison alcohol was for me.

The Final Experiment

I also spent a good amount of time sober during those eight months. It was the first extended period of sobriety for me in years. And like the guilt-ridden drinking bouts, I learned a lot about myself while sober. I learned what it would be like to wake up refreshed and able to work on myself. I got to see what it was like to go a whole week without a hangover. I lost quite a bit of weight during this time, so it showed me how quickly my body would repair if I simply kicked the drink.

So during my eight-month trial period, I saw both sides: I witnessed the horrors of what continued drinking would mean for me, and I got to experience how much better life would be if I stopped. And after eight months of slip-ups, learning, and struggle, I was able to commit. I haven't had a drink since, and I haven't so much as wanted one. And that was over two years ago.

My point is not only that slip-ups are part of the game, but that they are a *necessary* part of the game. If I didn't struggle during those eight months, I wouldn't have learned many of the things that have led me to where I am today. It was during those depressing times that I found books like *Kick the Drink* that have helped to form the foundation of my current mindset. It was during some of my darkest hours that I turned to meditation, and was able to see the power in that practice. If I had just been able to quit right away, I wouldn't have dug as deep as I did. Honestly, I couldn't be happier that it took me eight months to commit. I credit my sobriety and lifestyle with it.

Strive for Progress, Not Perfection

I hope that this book allows you to commit quicker than I was able to. That's why I wrote it. To teach you some of the things I learned through trial and error, and to show you the SoberPower Method, so that you never feel like you're in a lose-lose situation with sobriety. But always remember that big changes take time, and massive progress requires pain. Don't beat yourself up for your mistakes. Use them as learning experiences, and try to figure out where you went wrong. Recommit to your SoberPractice. Open up to your family and friends about the situation, and be honest with yourself. What did drinking do for you this time? Did it improve your life in any way? Are you any healthier or any closer to your goals?

I think that mistakes and slip-ups are required to truly commit to this lifestyle. So be thankful that they happen, but move on from them as quickly as possible. Alcohol is a terribly addictive drug that has most likely done quite a bit of damage to you. It wouldn't take much for you to go back to your old ways. But it also doesn't take much to get back on the SoberPower path. So pick yourself up the next day. Do you SoberPractice. Move on with a clear conscience. And enjoy the journey by making it about progress, not perfection.

I wish you the best as you gain your SoberPowers. You are worth every one of them.

Good luck.

You got this.